# THE GREAT
# SNAPE
# DEBATE

The Harry Potter books are supposed to be about Harry Potter. So why can't we stop talking about Severus Snape?

Love him or love to hate him, Snape has become *the* pivotal character in the Harry Potter series. There are plenty of reasons to believe he killed Dumbledore at the end of *Half-Blood Prince* at Dumbledore's behest—but plenty of reasons not to, too. So is Snape on Harry's side, or is he on Voldemort's? Is he bad to the bone, or just a little misunderstood?

Only after *Deathly Hallows* will we know for sure . . . but we can make some educated guesses now. In *The Great Snape Debate*, you'll get all the facts on our favorite Potions Master so you can decide for yourself. . . .

*The Case*

*for*

*Snape's*
*Innocence*

# THE GREAT
# SNAPE
# DEBATE

*Is Snape Harry Potter's Friend?*

AMY BERNER

ORSON SCOTT CARD

JOYCE MILLMAN

exclusive

Developed for Borders, Inc., by BenBella Books, Inc.
Send feedback to feedback@benbellabooks.com

Printed in the United States of America
10 9 8 7 6 5 4 3 2 1

Library of Congress Cataloging-in-Publication Data is available for this title.

Proofreading by Jennifer Thomason and Yara Abuata
Cover design by Mondolithic Studios, Inc.
Text design and composition by Laura Watkins
Printed by Victor Graphics, Inc.

*To everyone who enjoys the spell that any good book can cast, and to all those who have cast a spell on me with their support, love, and friendship*
—Amy Berner

*To all the nonreaders who became readers because of the Harry Potter books*
—Orson Scott Card

*To my husband and son, for their support*
—Joyce Millman

# The Case for Snape's Innocence

(For the Case for Snape's Guilt, flip over this book)

# I.

# IN DEFENSE OF SNAPE

SEVERUS SNAPE KILLED ALBUS DUMBLEDORE. He pointed his wand directly at him, shouted, "*Avada Kedavra!*," and killed him. Dead. End of story, right? Nope, not by a long shot.

The debate began the moment readers closed their copies of *Half-Blood Prince*. Did Snape kill Dumbledore on Dumbledore's orders? Whose side is Professor Snape really on? Through six books, J. K. Rowling has cast a shadow of doubt over Snape's every action, whether good or bad. She has painted Snape not in black or white, but in shades of gray. He is one of the most inscrutable characters in all of literature, which is why it's so tempting to try to unravel the mystery of his true nature. And so much fun.

# Part I: The Potterverse Evidence

As far as this essay is concerned, Snape is loyal to Dumbledore. He has been loyal all along and was carrying out Dumbledore's orders when he killed him. Those on the other side of the debate are probably asking (with good reason), "How can you see what happened and not believe it?" Well, with J. K. Rowling, what you see is not always what you get. You need to read the Harry Potter saga with two pairs of eyes: one to absorb the story and the other to seek out what might be happening between the lines. First, we'll examine the evidence for Snape's loyalty to Dumbledore from the factual perspective, looking at events and actions as they take place in the books (the "Potterverse"). Later, we'll switch to a literary perspective to find hidden evidence of Snape's allegiance to Dumbledore in the themes, devices, and word choices Rowling uses to tell her story.

### Snape's Actions throughout the Books

There are five key indications that Snape is one of the good guys:

- He expresses remorse to Dumbledore over the death of Lily and James Potter and turns spy for Dumbledore before Lord Voldemort's fall
- He prevents Voldemort from obtaining the Sorcerer's Stone (*Sorcerer's Stone*)
- He does not go to the graveyard immediately when summoned by

the Dark Mark upon Voldemort's return (*Goblet of Fire*), but goes only after being ordered to by Dumbledore

- He does not join Voldemort's Death Eaters against Dumbledore's Order of the Phoenix in the battle at the Ministry of Magic (*Order of the Phoenix*)
- He saves Harry from the Death Eaters at the end of *Half-Blood Prince*

In addition to the above list, there are many other hints in the Potterverse that Snape is loyal to Dumbledore. Snape appears in the imposter Mad-Eye Moody's Foe Glass (indicating he is a foe of Voldemort, since the false Moody was a Death Eater) in *Goblet of Fire*. He alerts the Order when Harry goes to the Ministry after seeing the vision of Sirius Black in trouble in *Order of the Phoenix*. In *Half-Blood Prince*, he treats Dumbledore's injuries after Dumbledore is burned destroying the Marvolo ring Horcrux. Also in *Half-Blood Prince*, he tries to find out when and how Draco Malfoy intends to carry out his plan to kill Dumbledore.

Also, while Snape has many opportunities to kill Harry, he does not. Instead, he protects him. He counteracts Professor Quirrell's spell to knock him off his broom during the Quidditch match in *Sorcerer's Stone*, and makes a rare appearance as a referee during a subsequent match in order to be closer to Harry. He gives Dolores Umbridge fake Veritaserum when she wants to interrogate Harry in *Order of the Phoenix*, and stalls when she asks him for a second batch. And he teaches Harry exactly the things he needs to know in order to survive the dangers at hand or to make sense of confusing events. (Whether or not Harry is paying attention is another issue.) On the first day of Potions class in *Sorcerer's Stone*, for example, Snape teaches the class that a bezoar (a stone found in the belly of a goat) is an antidote to most kinds of poisoning; a bezoar later figures prominently in *Half-Blood Prince*. In *Chamber of Secrets*, Snape introduces the class to Polyjuice Potion, which comes into play in that book, as well as in *Goblet of Fire* and *Half-Blood Prince*. He gives Harry Occlumency lessons (*Order of the Phoenix*) in an attempt to teach him to close his mind to Voldemort. In *Half-Blood Prince*, as the Defense Against the Dark Arts teacher, Snape stresses the importance of non-verbal spells and combat, which Harry could have benefited from at the climax of the book. Snape is still teaching Harry in his last moments in

*Half-Blood Prince*; as Harry and Snape are fighting, Snape shouts at him, "'Blocked again and again and again until you learn to keep your mouth shut and your mind closed, Potter!'" (603).

And Snape teaches and protects Harry even though he obviously dislikes him. Snape picks on Harry and cruelly singles him out for criticism and punishment—payback for the torment Snape suffered at the hands of James Potter back in their days as students at Hogwarts. In *Sorcerer's Stone* we learn from Dumbledore that James and Snape were adversaries similar to Harry and Draco. But James saved Snape from being attacked by Remus Lupin in werewolf state, after a prank intended to lure Snape into the Shrieking Shack went wrong. And that made the proud Snape hate James even more. How mortifying to have to be rescued by your archrival, especially when you suspect he was only doing it to avoid being expelled from school himself! And how frustrating to be reminded of that humiliating event after all this time by the presence of your archrival's look-alike son. But when one wizard saves another's life, he is owed a debt. Dumbledore explains that the reason Snape worked so hard to protect Harry was because he wanted to clear the balance sheet with James, as quickly as possible. That Snape felt obliged to repay the life debt, even with all the bad blood between him and James, suggests that Snape is a man of honor. He might be a sinister, ill-tempered creep, but that doesn't make him incapable of doing the right thing.

As for Snape's actions at the climax of *Half-Blood Prince*, if you believe Snape is loyal to Dumbledore, then you have to believe that Dumbledore's death was part of a plan between the two wizards. This theory is supported by the following points:

- Snape isn't aware that Draco and the Death Eaters have begun the attack on Hogwarts, suggesting that Snape never succeeded in finding out the details of Draco's plan
- Snape does not kill Professor Flitwick when he has the opportunity, only stuns him, and he does not kill or harm Hermione and Luna when he comes out of his office and sees them there
- At the climax of *Half-Blood Prince*, Dumbledore says "'Severus'" in a "pleading" manner. Rowling tells us that Snape gazes "for a moment at Dumbledore" before killing him (595). That's moment enough for some nonverbal communication to pass between them

# The Case for Snape's Innocence

We'll take a closer look at the evidence that suggests Snape killed Dumbledore on Dumbledore's orders in the section "The Smoking Wand."

## Dumbledore Trusts Snape

The case for Snape's innocence revolves around Dumbledore. He is Rowling's wise mentor figure in the saga and his trust in Snape carries considerable weight. In *Half-Blood Prince*, Dumbledore tells Harry that he believes Snape's remorse is genuine and that the death of James and Lily is "'the greatest regret'" of Snape's life (549). Dumbledore reiterates his faith in Snape throughout the series, and only hours before he dies, tells Harry, "'I trust Severus Snape completely'" (549). Dumbledore's trust in Snape also influences the way other usually reliable characters feel about him; Hermione and Professor Lupin both say that their faith in Dumbledore's judgment overrules whatever reservations they might have about the Potions Master's loyalties.

Could Dumbledore have been wrong about Snape? Of course. We see Dumbledore making mistakes throughout the series, as in *Goblet of Fire*, when he fails to recognize that Mad-Eye Moody is not who he claims to be. And, in *Order of the Phoenix*, he asks Snape to give Harry Occlumency lessons, with disastrous results, misjudging Snape's ability to put his hatred of James behind him.

But on the other hand, in *Half-Blood Prince*, Dumbledore makes an important distinction between his judgment of Snape and his judgment of Tom Riddle: he tells Harry that he never made the mistake of believing Riddle was trustworthy. And yet, he trusts Snape, even though, as a student, Snape was as obsessed with the Dark Arts as Riddle had been. So Dumbledore must see something in Snape that we can't. Dumbledore also readily acknowledges Snape's shortcomings (his cold and intimidating manner, his grudge against Harry), but he separates Snape's personality problems from the issue of trust. This all suggests that Dumbledore has made a carefully reasoned decision to trust Snape, despite his history as a follower of Voldemort and his general unpleasantness. However, we are missing the crucial piece of information needed to fully understand why Dumbledore trusts Snape "'completely'" (549) — the "'iron-clad reason'" (616) as Professor McGonagall calls it in *Half-Blood Prince*. More on what Dumbledore may be holding back in later sections.

A persuasive indication of Dumbledore's trust, and of Snape's loyalty, appears in *Half-Blood Prince*, when Dumbledore asks for Snape after drinking the poison in the cave. "'It is . . . Professor Snape whom I need . . .'" he tells Harry (580). This suggests that there was some kind of plan or agreement in place between Dumbledore and Snape; otherwise, why not request Professor Slughorn, who, as the current Potions Master, would have been just as capable as Snape of mixing an antidote for Voldemort's poison? It seems that Dumbledore trusted Snape with his life: to take it, as well as to save it. You can't trust anybody more than that.

### Voldemort Does Not Trust Snape

There is no point in arguing that Snape has fooled Voldemort, who is as powerful and smart a wizard as they come. Snape has *not* fooled Voldemort. From evidence in the Potterverse, it seems likely that Voldemort knows Snape is loyal to Dumbledore, and has known this for a long time. He might have had his suspicions ever since Snape gave him incomplete information about Trelawney's prophecy and Voldemort was nearly destroyed trying to kill the infant Harry. After the attack backfired on him, Voldemort had a lot of time to nurture suspicion about Snape's loyalty. Maybe he thinks Snape knew more than he told him and set him up. Maybe he suspects that Snape was working for Dumbledore at the time he heard the prophecy, though as far as we've been told, he was not. Whatever the reason, Voldemort began to doubt Snape, and those doubts grew.

Rowling gives us no direct evidence that Voldemort trusts Snape. We never see Snape and Voldemort together, the way we see Snape and Dumbledore together, so we can't judge for ourselves. And, unlike Dumbledore, Voldemort never talks about trusting Snape. The only reference Voldemort makes to Snape's loyalty (or lack of it) at all is in the graveyard scene of *Goblet of Fire*, when he characterizes a missing and unnamed Death Eater—whom we later learn from Death Eater Bellatrix Lestrange in *Half-Blood Prince* was Snape—as "'[o]ne, who I believe has left me forever . . . he will be killed . . .'" (651). That's not exactly a ringing endorsement.

In the "Spinner's End" chapter of *Half-Blood Prince*, Bellatrix asks Snape to explain his suspicious actions (preventing Quirrell from obtaining the Sorcerer's Stone, not returning to Voldemort immediately when he was resurrected, not revealing the whereabouts of the Order's headquarters, his absence from the Ministry battle, not killing Harry when he had the chance, and being so cozily settled at Hogwarts under Dumbledore's protection). Snape tells her that he has already been called on the carpet by Voldemort to discuss those very issues, and asks, "'Do you really think that, had I not been able to give satisfactory answers, I would be sitting here talking to you?'" (26). Whoa, not so fast, Professor! If Voldemort trusted you, why did he send Wormtail to be your new roommate? Clearly, Voldemort can't be as satisfied with Snape's answers as Snape claims he is, if he has Wormtail spying on him from behind staircase doors.

The fact that Voldemort has allowed Snape to continue his charade of loyalty doesn't necessarily mean Voldemort believes him. It could mean that Voldemort does *not* believe him, and is toying with him. Judging by the litany of excuses Snape recites in answer to Bellatrix's questions, he has not been much of a spy for Voldemort. What has he actually delivered? Voldemort would have to be a monumental dunce to believe Snape's lame excuse that he remained under Dumbledore's protection at Hogwarts for all those years because he was maintaining his post as the Dark Lord's spy. Voldemort could have (should have?) reduced Snape to a smoldering pile of ash by now, and yet, with all his suspicions, he hasn't. Why? Not because he trusts him (the Dark Lord didn't get where he is by trusting people), but because he has been biding his time. He's figuring out how best to use Snape before killing him in the most painful way possible. And there is the chilling possibility that Voldemort has found an elegantly diabolical benefit to his Snape problem: He can use him to get rid of Dumbledore.

## The Unbreakable Vow

Snape is repeatedly described as a highly skilled Legilimens and Occlumens. But is he really as good as we are led to believe? Perhaps not. In *Order of the Phoenix*, Harry manages to get past him and see a few childhood memories. In *Half-Blood Prince* Snape apparently tries to use Legilimency on Draco to find out his plan, but can't—Aunt Bellatrix taught him Occlumency. Snape tells Harry during their Occlumency lessons in *Order of the Phoenix* that Voldemort is an expert Legilimens who "'almost always knows when'" someone is lying (531). Note that "almost." So maybe Voldemort has been able to use Legilimens on Snape to determine his true loyalty, despite what Snape may believe. (This, of course, means that Dumbledore might also have been able to get past Snape's defenses—and he keeps saying that he trusts him, so what does that tell you?)

Or maybe it's a simple matter of Voldemort calling Snape's bluff, without any mind-violating at all. Snape repeats to Bellatrix the "satisfactory" answer he gave Voldemort when questioned why Dumbledore trusts him so much: Snape told the Dark Lord that he spun Dumbledore "'a tale of deepest remorse'" over the death of James and Lily (*Half-Blood Prince* 31). If you've watched any movies or TV series about undercover agents, you know that a good cover story is always based in truth; it helps spies maintain their own beliefs in the roles they're playing. Perhaps Voldemort suspects that Snape's remorse is genuine, and he wants to test his suspicions. Here is one plausible scenario: Voldemort orders Draco's mother, Narcissa Malfoy, to go to Snape and trap him into promising to kill Dumbledore himself if it appears that Draco will fail. Voldemort would have used Draco as collateral, promising (perhaps emptily) his safety if Narcissa complied and threatening to kill them both if she didn't. That's just the kind of guy Voldemort is. And maybe Snape is able to perform Legilimens on Narcissa during her visit (there are a lot of long looks between them), and so he knows all this. She may even want him to know; it makes her situation even more sympathetic.

The dilemma Snape faces here—he has the fate of a mother and child in his hands—closely mirrors the part Snape played in the fate of Lily and Harry. Voldemort is preying on Snape's emotional weakness—the very one that Snape handed him in the guise of an undercover spy's true lie. The Dark Lord is betting that Snape is so guilt-ridden over what he did to the Potters that he will not be able to refuse the chance to alleviate his conscience by protecting another family from death at Voldemort's hands. (If this scenario is correct, it also proves that Snape's remorseful declaration to Dumbledore is genuine.)

When Narcissa delivers her request for the Unbreakable Vow, it catches Snape off guard. You can tell how surprised he is from the way he stalls for time, repeating the words, "'Unbreakable Vow?'" (*Half-Blood Prince* 35). Bellatrix laughs at him. Snape knows he is on thin ice, that he has not put to rest Bellatrix's suspicions. Bellatrix, after all, is a highly respected member of the Death Eater community, even if she's fallen somewhat out of favor with Voldemort since the events at the end of *Order of the Phoenix*.

Snape must agree to this flamboyant act in order to prove his "loyalty" to Voldemort and continue as Dumbledore's spy—although it's doubtful, at this point, that Snape really believes anymore that Voldemort trusts him. And, while making the vow, Snape's hand twitches, as if his body is betraying his unwillingness. He knows he is in deep, deep trouble.

## The Smoking Wand: The Scene That Proves Snape Killed Dumbledore on Dumbledore's Orders

In *Half-Blood Prince*, Hagrid informs Harry that he came upon Snape and Dumbledore arguing in the forest. "'I jus' heard Snape sayin' Dumbledore took too much for granted an' maybe he—Snape—didn' wan' ter do it anymore,'" reports Hagrid. "'Dumbledore told him flat out he'd agreed ter do it an' that was all there was to it'" (405–406).

In light of the mess Snape got himself into in "Spinner's End," isn't it likely that Dumbledore and Snape were arguing about the Unbreakable Vow problem, and about a related plan or agreement made between them? Here's what might have happened: Snape went to Dumbledore after making the Unbreakable Vow with Narcissa. They mulled over their options. Maybe Snape wanted to try to come up with some spell or potion to undo the vow, maybe they discussed hiding Draco and Narcissa in some kind of wizard witness protection program, as Dumbledore offers Draco himself at the end of *Half-Blood Prince*. They've gone around and around and they're at a loss. They don't know the details of Draco's plan or when he will attack. Maybe Snape wanted to break the vow, even if it meant his own death. But Dumbledore tells him their priorities. They have to protect Harry. They have to protect Draco; they know that Voldemort expects Draco to die trying to kill Dumbledore—this is Lucius Malfoy's punishment for failing to retrieve the prophecy from the Ministry of Magic—and Dumbledore will not allow this to happen. They have to protect Snape's appearance of loyalty to Voldemort for as long as it takes Harry to become mature enough to kill Voldemort and survive—thus ensuring that Harry will have Snape as an ally positioned within Voldemort's camp (if Snape lives that long). And if, in pursuing these goals, events unfold in a way that means that Snape has to kill Dumbledore, then so be it.

Snape does not want to agree to this. Hagrid hears him tell Dumbledore that he takes too much for granted—which could mean, among other

9

things, that Dumbledore takes the security of Snape's position within Voldemort's circle for granted. If the Dark Lord is onto him anyway, Snape might be reasoning, they don't need to play out the hand he's dealt them. But, as Hagrid overhears it, Dumbledore is "'[p]retty firm'" with Snape, and tells him he has to stick to the agreement (*Half-Blood Prince* 406).

If it's true that this argument was about Snape's Unbreakable Vow with Narcissa, then it's further evidence of Snape's loyalty to Dumbledore. If Snape is loyal to Voldemort, why would he tell Dumbledore about the vow and Draco's plan? Wouldn't he just keep his mouth shut and let it all happen?

There has been speculation among fans that Snape could have had an Unbreakable Vow with Dumbledore as well as with Narcissa. And this Unbreakable Vow could have been part of a plan to fake Dumbledore's death, or it could have something to do with the "'ironclad reason'" why Dumbledore trusts Snape. However, the possibility of an Unbreakable Vow between those two seems doubtful, considering what we know about Dumbledore and the manner in which he judges people. We're told that Dumbledore "'has to believe the best of people'" (*Half-Blood Prince* 31); he seems to rely on his own internal radar in deciding who is trustworthy. Sometimes he is wrong. But from what we've seen of his unfailingly ethical and civil behavior, it seems like asking someone to make an Unbreakable Vow is just not his style. That's more the style of someone consumed with suspicion, someone who expects the worst from people—someone like Voldemort. It's likely that Dumbledore would consider asking for an Unbreakable Vow to be an insult to a person's integrity. Dumbledore would instead ask for a person's word (as we see him do with Harry in the cave) and expect that her or she will honor this agreement. And we know that Snape is a man of honor, from the way he works to pay off that life debt to James.

Perhaps Dumbledore and Snape reached a compromise about what they would do if Draco attempted to assassinate the headmaster. They might have agreed to look for another way out until the last possible second. Evidence: In the climactic scene, as Draco is holding Dumbledore at wandpoint, Dumbledore tells him that they could fake his (Draco's) death and keep his mother safe.

But, if it became necessary for Snape to kill him, then Dumbledore might have insisted that he was to do so without hesitation. In order to level an Unforgivable Curse and have it succeed, you have to mean it.

You have to access the "right" emotions in the right quantity. Dumbledore trusts Snape to follow this order because he knows that the unsentimental, rigidly compartmentalized Snape would not let the "wrong" emotions get in the way of what needed to be done.

Some fans who believe Snape is innocent theorize that Snape and Dumbledore faked Dumbledore's death. There's only one problem with this theory. When it was presented to Rowling by author Salman Rushdie (a pretty good storyteller in his own right) and his young son during a public question-and-answer session with Rowling at Radio City Music Hall in August 2006, Rowling's response was, "Dumbledore is definitely dead." (She didn't, however, say anything about whether he's going to stay that way. . . .)

So, we come to the face-off between Dumbledore and Draco, with Harry watching from the sidelines while wrapped in the Invisibility Cloak and placed under an immobilizing spell by Dumbledore. (Clearly, Dumbledore does not want Harry to interfere in whatever transpires, which further suggests that he was following a plan.) Four Death Eaters arrive before Snape does, and start making noises about Draco not having the nerve to kill Dumbledore. This is a serious complication; perhaps Dumbledore and Snape were planning to hide Draco and have Snape go back to Voldemort with a tale of how Draco died attempting to carry out the Dark Lord's order. But now, these other Death Eaters are unanticipated witnesses who will report everything to Voldemort. Meanwhile, Dumbledore is suffering from unbearable psychic and physical pain from the potion he drank in the cave; he likely believes the poison is going to be fatal. And then Snape bursts on the scene. He sees the other Death Eaters preparing to finish off Dumbledore, and maybe Draco as well. Dumbledore and Snape both know that they have to act fast. Dumbledore is not pleading for his life when he says "Severus," he is pleading for Snape to honor their agreement and kill him. There is a moment of silence before Snape complies—enough time for some non-verbal communication (an order? A goodbye? A counter-spell?) to pass between them.

### The Lily Potter Factor

Throughout the series, Snape never insults Lily, although he's always trashing James. Snape never even insults Lily by association, as in "your parents were obnoxious" — it is always just "your father." We can safely conclude that Snape hated James, but there is no evidence that he hated Lily.

In *Half-Blood Prince*, we learn that Lily excelled at Potions. Professor Slughorn tells Harry that she was the best student he'd ever seen, that she had an "'instinctive'" grasp of the subject (319). Slughorn also mentions that he taught Snape in Potions and that he was no slouch, either. Given this information, it's possible that, despite being in different Houses, and despite Snape being very much the outcast and Lily the popular girl, Snape and Lily formed some kind of bond over their mutual talent for potion-making. This doesn't mean they were boyfriend-and-girlfriend (although Snape, like so many other boys in their class, might have had a crush on her), but, simply, friends. (And how many female friends do you think the socially awkward "Snivellus" had in high school? Lily could have been the only one.) There is even some possible evidence in *Half-Blood Prince* that the spells scrawled in the margins of Snape's old Potions textbook could have been collaborations with Lily, or Lily's alone. Hermione thinks the Half-Blood Prince's handwriting looks like a girl's, and there are similarities between the bezoar instructions in the margins of the textbook, Lily's maverick use of the bezoar (as recounted by Slughorn), and what Snape teaches the class about the bezoar back in *Sorcerer's Stone*.

But what about the "Snape's Worst Memory" chapter from *Order of the Phoenix*, in which Harry sees Snape's teenage memory of being humiliated and bullied by James? James has Snape hanging upside down with his underpants exposed, and Lily comes along and tells him to leave Snape alone. When James does let Snape down, Snape says he doesn't need help from a "'Mudblood'" like Lily (and she gets mad at him and makes a rude remark about the dingy state of his drawers) (648). Some have taken this as an indication that Snape hated Lily. But think about what's going on in this scene and you'll see that it's a very credible depiction of typical adolescent behavior: the bullying, the boys showing off for the popular girl, the popular girl not wanting to seem too friendly with the school weirdo, the mercurial emotions of teenagers. There's a believable tension between Snape and Lily in this scene as well. She rescues him (possibly because of their secret friendship); he is embarrassed about being rescued by a girl, especially someone he probably has a little crush on. Not to mention, she saw his underpants. Under these circumstances, we should not take Snape's "'Mudblood'" epithet as any reliable indication that he hates Lily. Nor should we take Lily's defensive mocking of his underpants as an indication that she hates Snape. Just look at the way the angry Lily and the teasing James spar with each other during the same Pensieve scene (and the way Ron and Hermione bicker throughout the series); it's only human to protect vulnerable feelings behind the appearance of their opposite.

Speaking of the underpants . . . James uses a nonverbal *Levicorpus* spell to hang Snape upside down. In the Half-Blood Prince's Potions textbook, Harry finds handwritten instructions for a nonverbal *Levicorpus* spell. If Lily and Snape were friends, they might have been experimenting with spells together or sharing their discoveries. And the added tension between Lily and Snape in the Pensieve scene could come from the fact that Snape believed Lily had taught James the nonverbal *Levicorpus* spell—their spell. Snape all but confirms this scenario at the climax of *Half-Blood Prince*, when Harry attempts to use the *Levicorpus* spell on Snape and Snape screams, "'You'd turn my inventions on me, like your filthy father, would you?'" (604).

If Snape and Lily had been friends, it proves Snape's remorse over her death is genuine. Dumbledore might even know of the depth of Snape's feelings for Lily, or of some bond or pact between them. But if Dumbledore did know something, he chose not to share it with Harry.

## Snape's Redemptive Path

The idea that Snape is struggling toward redemption is popular with readers who believe in his innocence. Like everything about Snape in the Potterverse, the evidence is ambiguous. It's all a matter of how we interpret Snape's actions. If we believe in Snape's loyalty, we can intuit Snape's desire for redemption from his turning spy for Dumbledore ("'at great personal risk'" [*Goblet of Fire* 591]), from his expression of remorse, from his protection of Harry, and from his work for the Order.

And, if we believe in Snape's loyalty to Dumbledore, we should consider for a moment what this loyalty requires of Snape. He is asked to protect the son of the bully who emotionally scarred him; spy on a mass-murdering despot, kill the man who took him in and gave him a second chance, and be reviled as a betrayer. And, oh yeah, Voldemort is probably going to *Crucio* him into the next century for thwarting his plan to

# Speculations

## What Do Snape's Boggart and Patronus Look Like?

J. K. Rowling has repeatedly declined to answer this question in interviews and fan Q&A sessions throughout the years, explaining that this information would give too much away. And she's probably right.

But we can speculate. In the Potterverse, a Boggart is the thing a person fears the most. So, what is Severus Snape most afraid of? The answer is simple: exposure. As a teenager, he was humiliated by James Potter, who held him upside down in the air with a *Levicorpus* spell so that his robes opened and his "graying underpants" and skinny, bare legs were on view to a crowd of laughing classmates (*Order of the Phoenix* 647). As a result, Snape has adopted a many-layered, tightly buttoned-up uniform in his adulthood. No part of his body shows except for his hands, a sliver of neck, and his head.

Snape is also a spy. Whether he's undercover for Dumbledore or undercover for Voldemort (or both), he cannot let his guard down and reveal his true loyalties and feelings.

Given all this, it seems fair to say that Snape's Boggart would be a manifestation of his fear of exposure. It's probably himself wearing only graying underpants.

Boggarts are repelled by the Riddikulus charm, which is conjured by concentrating on a funny thought. What funny thought would Snape use to make his Boggart disappear? James Potter turned upside down in *his* underpants, of course.

Snape's Patronus, on the other hand, is more difficult to imagine. The Patronus is a shield against Dementors, powered by a person's single happiest memory. Has Snape ever been happy? This is open to debate. But since he's a powerful wizard, we have to assume that he can indeed conjure a Patronus. So there must be some happy memory buried in the dark recesses of the Snapean psyche. And this memory must be loaded with spoilers, or Rowling would have revealed it by now. A wild guess: Lily Potter.

have Draco die attempting to kill Dumbledore. Only someone with a serious commitment to atonement would agree to a deal like that. And there's even more evidence that Snape could be headed for redemption in the next part of our case, which looks at the evidence for his innocence in the way Rowling has chosen to tell her story.

# Part II: The Literary Case for Snape's Innocence

There are no coincidences in fiction. The Harry Potter saga is J. K. Rowling's world, and every character, event, word, and punctuation mark she puts into it is there for a reason. Of course, only Rowling knows for sure where the story is headed. But we can make like Professor Trelawney and read the tea leaves. The evidence for Snape's innocence is concealed in the word choices, recurring themes, and storytelling devices and patterns Rowling uses. It reveals itself in what's not said, as well as what's said. Rowling can't afford to be obvious, because the momentum of the entire series depends on Snape remaining as ambiguous as possible for as long as possible. That we are still able to debate Snape's loyalties after six books is testament to how expertly Rowling has done her job.

## *Looks Can Be Deceiving*

Rowling has made Harry present as a witness to all but a small portion of the action in books one through six. We are seeing the story from his perspective. But Harry wears glasses, and glasses are frequently used in literature as a metaphor for lack of insight or understanding. Rowling is telling us that Harry is an unreliable witness.

Indeed, Harry is often in the dark, literally and figuratively, when major events happen. He misunderstands what he sees; he only has part of the information he needs to correctly interpret events; he is veiled behind the Invisibility Cloak; unconscious; dreaming; or seeing false images planted in his mind. And Harry fails to read people correctly. He initially mistakes Sirius as an enemy and the fake Moody as a friend.

Nowhere is Harry's selective blindness more important than in his attitude toward Snape. Harry interprets every act of Snape's as malevolent. His vision becomes more and more clouded by what Lupin terms the "prejudice" against Snape that Harry inherited from James and Sirius. To be fair to Harry, Snape started it; he tormented Harry from the moment they met in Potions class.

Harry takes Snape's malevolence at face value, and you can't blame him. Rowling has drawn Snape with all the characteristics of the classic villain. She describes him as "cruel" (*Chamber of Secrets* 77), "hook-nosed," and "sallow" (*Sorcerer's Stone* 126). He is clad from head to toe in sinister black. He sneers, he slithers. Looking into his "cold" black eyes is like looking into "dark tunnels" (*Sorcerer's Stone* 136). Throughout the series, Rowling creates a pattern of Harry always suspecting Snape of the misdeed of the hour, sometimes to the point where that suspicion nearly costs him his life at the hands of the real culprit (Quirrell in *Sorcerer's Stone*, fake Moody in *Goblet of Fire*). The lesson that Rowling is teaching here (and that Harry has yet to learn) is that you should not judge people on appearance and temperament alone. Snape is thoroughly unpleasant, but even unpleasant people can do noble things. For contrast, Rowling gives us the heroically handsome Gilderoy Lockhart, who is a coward and a fraud; the motherly Dolores Umbridge, who is a fanatical tyrant; and the gruff but friendly Moody, who isn't even Moody. *Are you sure you want to take Snape at face value?* Rowling is whispering to us (and Harry), all the while making the git as wonderfully greasy as possible.

### Snape the Shapeshifter

Rowling masterfully cloaks Snape in ambiguity. As we have examined in the Potterverse argument, Rowling offers contradictory explanations and mitigating circumstances for Snape's every action, in order to mask his true loyalty and motives. Yes, he is mean to Harry (but James was mean to Snape). Yes, we see him leveling the Killing Curse at Dumbledore (but Dumbledore trusted him).

The enigmatic figure is not a new one in literature, nor is the kind of heroic quest that Harry is on. Both are as old as time itself. In his influential book *The Hero with a Thousand Faces*, mythology scholar Joseph Campbell showed how all mythologies, religious gospels, and folk tales of heroism across cultures and throughout time are essentially the same. The story of Buddha, the story of Jesus, the story of Moses, the story of Mohammed, and the stories of Odysseus and King Arthur all follow a similar pattern, which Campbell called the "Monomyth," or "The Hero's Adventure."

As Campbell described it in an interview with Bill Moyers in the book *The Power of Myth*, the hero's adventure "begins with someone from whom something has been taken, or who feels there's something lacking in the normal experiences available or permitted. . . . This person then takes off on a series of adventures beyond the ordinary, either to recover what has been lost or to discover some life-giving elixir. It's usually a cycle, a going and a returning" (152). The hero initially refuses, but then accepts his destiny, and throughout his journey, undergoes trials in which he learns the meaning of sacrifice and gains enlightenment. In his work, Campbell built upon psychologist Carl Jung's "archetypes"—patterns of personality common throughout the human race—to populate the Monomyth with the allies, enemies, mentors, spiritual guides, and others whom the hero meets along the way.

The most famous disciple of Joseph Campbell is director George Lucas, who was inspired by *The Hero with a Thousand Faces* in making Star Wars. More recently, writer Christopher Vogler published *The Writer's Journey*, in which he traced Campbell's Monomyth through the Star Wars movies, as well as other films, such as *The Matrix* and The Lord of the Rings trilogy. Vogler further examined the archetypes that show up in all these movies; the list includes the Hero, the Mentor, and the Shadow Self, the character who represents the buried but tempting dark side of the Hero's personality. According to Vogler, another important archetype common to all popular mythologies is the Shapeshifter, who "serves the dramatic function of bringing doubt and suspense into the story" regarding his loyalty (67). The Shapeshifter can initially present himself as neutral, good, or bad, but he switches sides at some point in the story. The Shapeshifter may mislead or confuse the Hero, who often doesn't know until the last moment whether the Shapeshifter is an ally or an enemy. As you can see, Snape is a Shapeshifter all the way. (Some other Shapeshifters are Cypher in *The Matrix*, Han Solo in the first Star Wars film, and history's most famous Shapeshifter, Judas. Although Darth Vader does sacrifice his own life to save Luke in *Return of the Jedi*, he is not a Shapeshifter. Vader is widely defined as the prime popular example of the Shadow Self; he is, after all, a part of Luke, being his father. Voldemort, who is physically connected to Harry by Harry's scar, is the Shadow Self in the Potter saga.)

17

The only satisfying payoff to all the ambiguity that Rowling has created around Snape is to have this ideal Shapeshifter shift. Indeed, the resolution of the plot demands that Snape unambiguously declare a side in Book Seven. Those who believe that Snape is on Voldemort's side might say that Snape did declare his loyalty, loud and clear, by killing Dumbledore. But if that's the case, and Snape has been loyal to Voldemort all along, it still means he is overdue for a shift from bad to good. Remember this important point: Rowling means for us to see the story through Harry's perspective. And Harry has never believed Snape's conversion, remorse, or loyalty, so Snape's killing of Dumbledore doesn't amount to any shift of Snape's loyalties from good to bad in Harry's eyes. (And you know you are not meant to trust Harry's eyes.) Note also the Shapeshifter's other purpose: to confuse the Hero. Harry has let it get personal between him and Snape; Rowling tells us in *Half-Blood Prince* that he now hates Snape as much as he hates Voldemort. Shapeshifter Snape is a distraction that Harry cannot afford.

### Decoding the Unbreakable Vow: Between the Lines of "Spinner's End"

Like any good writer, Rowling employs various literary devices to plant clues and draw attention to particular points. One favorite trick of Rowling's is the use of the well-meaning but loose-lipped Hagrid as a messenger to deliver unadorned clues that she wants us to ponder (and Harry to misread). In *Half-Blood Prince*, Hagrid delivers the "smoking wand" evidence that Snape was following Dumbledore's orders when he killed him by repeating an argument he overhears in the forest between Snape and Dumbledore, in which Snape tries to withdraw from an (unspecified) agreement and Dumbledore, being "'[p]retty firm'" with him, doesn't let him.

The forest argument is another example of how Rowling propels the plot by withholding crucial information and ensuring that Harry remains half in the dark. Falling back on his pattern of bias against Snape, Harry predictably interprets the argument as evidence that Dumbledore does not trust Snape after all. Withholding key information is also how Rowling enhances Snape's ambiguity and, most of all, how she springs surprises on us. We saw this previously in *Order of the Phoenix*, when Harry was told only that Trelawney's prophecy was overheard; later, in *Half-Blood Prince*, Rowling drops the bombshell that it was Snape who overheard the prophecy, and gave Voldemort the information that led to the death of Harry's parents.

The "Spinner's End" chapter of *Half-Blood Prince* is the finest example of how the manner in which Rowling tells her story is as important as the story itself. This chapter, in which Snape is visited in his home by Narcissa Malfoy and her sister, Death Eater Bellatrix Lestrange, is the only chapter in the series in which Rowling allows us to see Snape through our own eyes, not through Harry's perspective. Rowling makes this change in style because she wants this chapter to stand out as a red flag to readers. And, indeed, the entire chapter could be viewed as a huge clue supporting Snape's loyalty to Dumbledore.

In "Spinner's End," Snape speaks for himself, in answer to Bellatrix's questions about the actions that throw his loyalty to Voldemort into question. These are the same actions we've cited in the Potterverse section as evidence of his loyalty to Dumbledore (not joining the Death Eaters in the battle at the Ministry, not coming to Voldemort at once when the Dark Mark burned, etc.). Rowling lets Snape, the master dissembler, spin his justifications. But as he does, she subtly places us in the position of Bellatrix, listening to him with skepticism. And his smooth answers sound a little too well-rehearsed, his suave attitude seems a little too affected, his boasts of closeness with Voldemort a little too incredible. Snape's entire manner suggests a performance—a performance by a spy loyal to Dumbledore, desperately trying to maintain his cover within Voldemort's ranks.

Throughout "Spinner's End," Rowling builds up the picture of Snape on the defensive. The chapter's title itself suggests tale-spinners, spiders, webs of deceit, and endgames. Not only does Snape have to deal with Bellatrix's suspicion, he knows that Voldemort doubts his loyalty as well. Voldemort's faithful servant Wormtail hovers in the background, listening at keyholes. And there is Snape's own admission that he has been called to account for his suspicious actions by Voldemort himself. Snape tells Bellatrix with a show of blasé smugness, "'The Dark Lord's initial displeasure . . . vanished entirely, I assure you, when I explained that I remained faithful . . . ,'" which is a hilariously understated and sarcastic line when you consider that Snape is probably leaving out a few small details of that meeting, like torture and groveling (28–29).

In the Potterverse section, we examined the evidence in "Spinner's End" that seems to prove that Voldemort does not trust Snape; we speculated that the Dark Lord has been able to get past Snape's Occlumency defenses to ascertain his true loyalties, or he is simply testing his suspicion that Snape's remorse over the death of the Potters is genuine. We examined the possibility that Voldemort has decided to use Snape to get rid of Dumbledore, with Narcissa and Draco as bait. From a "Snape is innocent" perspective, the symmetry of Rowling suddenly throwing Narcissa and Draco into the mix makes sense. Having Narcissa beg Snape to protect her child from Voldemort is almost a replay of the situation upon which Snape's remorse and regret is supposedly based—his responsibility for the death of Lily and James (but, let's face it, mostly Lily) as they tried to protect Harry.

The way Rowling writes "Spinner's End" supports this theory. There are two separate conversations going on throughout the chapter, one between Snape and Bellatrix and one between Snape and Narcissa. Rowling gives us many tense descriptions of Snape looking into Narcissa's eyes, yet looking away from Bellatrix; it's clear that Snape and Narcissa are having private, nonverbal communication that Bellatrix is not part of, whether Legilimency is being employed or not. As we theorized before, Snape may have learned, from performing Legilimency on Narcissa, that Voldemort has forced her to come to him, and that Voldemort threatened Draco's life and her own if she did not comply. (It would seem, also, then, that Narcissa has not shared this threat with her sister, who knows only that the Dark Lord has assigned Draco a glorious task.)

Consider how Rowling describes Snape's reaction as Narcissa raises the issue of Snape killing Dumbledore instead of Draco doing the job, as Voldemort decreed. Rowling tells us that Snape is looking at Narcissa and "slowly" saying, "'He intends me to do it in the end, I think'" (34). This description of Snape's behavior differs sharply from his quick answers and almost-mocking suaveness earlier in the chapter. That use of the word "slowly" suggests that Snape is thinking on his feet; it could be that he is seeing Voldemort's true intentions for the first time, and realizing that he is a pawn in the Dark Lord's game. At this point, Snape is probably thinking that he and Dumbledore can come up with a way out, maybe fake a few deaths. And then Narcissa (maybe on Voldemort's orders) asks for the Unbreakable Vow.

Rowling suggests that Snape has been blindsided by Narcissa's request—she has Snape repeat, "'The Unbreakable Vow?'" (35). She also tells us that his face is "blank, unreadable" (35). This creates the image of Snape stalling and trying to keep his mind closed to Bellatrix (who, Rowling implies later in the book through Snape's conversation with Draco, is a pretty good Occlumens, so she must be a capable Legilimens as well). But Bellatrix may have sensed something in his hesitation, because she lets out a cackle of belittling laughter and says that Snape would never agree to a vow—which speaks volumes about what the prevailing level of trust in Snape must be among the Death Eaters. Rowling describes Snape as avoiding Bellatrix's eyes and instead, looking steadily into "Narcissa's tear-filled blue ones"—she is telling us that Snape is reading Narcissa (36). He could be seeing that Voldemort forced her to ask for the Unbreakable Vow. But, even if Narcissa is acting on her own, Snape has no choice but to consent; refusing would endanger the lives of Draco and Narcissa, and further damage his credibility with Bellatrix and the other Voldemort loyalists.

"Spinner's End" is a dazzling performance from Rowling. She maintains Snape's ambiguity with a chain of images that form a circular argument—Voldemort might or might not trust him, so maybe that means he's Dumbledore's man, but then he makes the Unbreakable Vow to kill Dumbledore, so he could be loyal to Voldemort after all. "'I have played my part well,'" Snape tells Bellatrix (31). But, despite all the doubt she casts in this chapter, Rowling also gives the case for innocence three of its most compelling arguments.

First, we see Snape showing compassion in wanting to help Narcissa and Draco. And if he can feel it here, it means that he could have felt it all those years ago with Lily, James, and Harry. It means that not only is his remorse genuine, it haunts him and he can't refuse this chance to succeed where he failed before. Second, would a Snape who was loyal to the Dark Lord agree to commit treason against him, which is what his agreement with Narcissa amounts to? Snape knows the consequences of disobedience; Voldemort "'does not forgive easily'" (34). (Yeah—or at all.) It's hard to believe that Snape would dare interfere with Voldemort's orders if he were loyal to him. And if he had nothing to hide, Snape wouldn't care how suspicious Bellatrix was about him, and wouldn't feel compelled to prove anything by making the Unbreakable Vow—not when it meant risking the wrath of Voldemort. Finally, Rowling tells us that, during the making of the Unbreakable Vow, Snape's hand twitches when Narcissa asks if he will "'carry out the deed that the Dark Lord has ordered Draco to perform?'" if it seems that Draco will fail (36). That tiny twitch is Rowling's way of show-ing us that Snape's body is betraying his unwillingness. He knows that Voldemort has caught him in his own web of lies, and he is doomed. The spider has become the fly.

## Lily and the Literary Case for Innocence

Rowling uses many of her favorite storytelling devices and mystery-build-ing tricks in her treatment of Lily Potter. She has not been generous with information about Lily, letting out only tidbits at a time. By contrast, we have a more vivid picture of James Potter, not the least because Harry hears so much about him from Snape, Sirius, and Lupin. In *Half-Blood Prince*, Rowling finally gives us the juicy detail that, as a student at Hogwarts, Lily excelled at Potions. As you remember from the Potterverse case for Snape's innocence, Lily's skill at Potions suggests that she and Snape could have developed a friendship over their mutual interest in the subject. At any rate, if Rowling remains true to this pattern of doling out information a little at a time only to shock us when she reveals the rest, she is saving a whopper of a revelation about Harry's mother for Book Seven.

Lily also figures in another of Rowling's trusted devices, misdirection—making readers think they're seeing something that they're not. In the Potterverse section about Lily, we examined how Harry assumes that Snape hated both his parents, but in reality, Snape did not, as far as we can tell, hate Lily. Rowling slyly directs our attention to this in *Half-Blood Prince*, when, after Snape kills Dumbledore, Harry tells Lupin that Dumbledore believed Snape's story of remorse over his parents' death. Lupin exclaims, "'Dumbledore believed Snape was sorry James was dead? Snape *hated* James . . .'" (616). Notice that Rowling cuts off Lupin at "James," and, indeed, leaves Lily out of the remarks entirely.

Moreover, as we saw in the Potterverse section, Snape never insults Lily, only James. In all the books, Snape never even utters Lily's name. Why? Because the feelings and memories Lily elicits are so painful—or powerful—that he has to act as if she never existed? "'The mind is a complex and many-layered thing, Potter,'" Snape says in the "Occlumency" chapter of *Order of the Phoenix* (530). This is Rowling reminding us that Snape is highly skilled at hiding and compartmental-izing his thoughts and emotions. How deep in those many layers has he hidden Lily, and why?

# The Case for Snape's Innocence

According to Dumbledore, Lily protected Harry from Voldemort's curse with a powerful ancient magic rooted in love. Additionally, in a scene that was invented for the *Prisoner of Azkaban* movie (with Rowling's approval), Lupin tells Harry about Lily's kindness, her extraordinary talent as a witch, and her "way of seeing the beauty in others, even, and perhaps most especially, when that person could not see it in themselves." In the same scene, Lupin tells Harry what we have heard so many times before—that he has his mother's eyes. What is this scene, and all of Rowling's references to Lily's eyes in the books, really telling us about Lily's "way of seeing"? Based on what we know about Lily's mastery of ancient magic, it's possible, even likely, that Lily's ability to see "the beauty in others" was more than a figure of speech. Could Lily "see" into people's hearts or souls? Was she an expert in an unnamed discipline along the lines of Legilimency, but different in that it does not look into the mind (which can be shut down or manipulated) but into the substance of a person, the heart and soul? Did Lily see the "beauty" in Snape, the potential for good, and did she share this observation with Dumbledore (but not with James, who would have scoffed at the idea of there being anything worthwhile about Snape)? Dumbledore also places great importance on love and "believ[ing] the best of people'" (*Half-Blood Prince* 31). Is Dumbledore's trust in Snape based on Lily's trust in Snape—and is this Dumbledore's "'ironclad reason'" for trusting Snape?

If this is true, then there is another question to ask: Does Harry have Lily's ability to "see"? Rowling certainly wants us to know that Harry has his mother's eyes—so many characters make this point throughout the books that it has become a running joke. Or a running clue. There are simply too many references to Harry's eyes being exactly like Lily's for Rowling to be talking only about their color. Remember, Rowling has given Harry eyeglasses; she uses his flawed sight as a metaphor for his flawed understanding. Given all this, it's reasonable to believe that Harry has inherited Lily's ability to see the truth of people's hearts, but either it hasn't kicked in yet or Harry is too blinded by his father's prejudices to employ it. (Remember that James, like Harry, wore glasses.) Dumbledore might have known of Lily's abilities, and the possibility that Harry has inherited them. (After all, Harry has inherited his father's talent for conjuring a Patronus, not to mention his skill at Quidditch.) Of the people left alive after *Half-Blood Prince*, it's possible that Lupin and

Snape also know how special Lily's eyes were. But the point is, Harry doesn't know. Considering Rowling's pattern of withholding information until she's ready to use it for maximum impact, we can assume that, if there is anything to this speculation about the true meaning of Harry having "his mother's eyes," it will play a major role in Book Seven. Specifically, it could play into Harry finally being able to see the truth about Snape's loyalty to Dumbledore.

### Snape and Harry: More Alike Than We Think

At the end of *Half-Blood Prince*, when Harry is telling Ron and Hermione about his plans to find the remaining Horcruxes and prepare for his showdown with Voldemort, Rowling writes the perfect line for a "coming attractions" trailer: "'[I]f I meet Severus Snape along the way,'" says Harry, "'so much the better for me, so much the worse for him'" (651). From a storytelling standpoint, it's not a question of "if" Harry will meet Snape again, but "when." The dramatic tension Rowling has created demands it; Snape and Harry are like two trains racing toward each other on the same track. On an emotional level, too, the saga demands that Snape and Harry resolve the unfinished business between them. Neither can complete their journey without the other's help.

For two people who supposedly loathe each other, Snape and Harry are surprisingly alike. Both are half-bloods. Both have been bullied. In *Half-Blood Prince*, Hermione notes that Snape's approach to teaching Defense Against the Dark Arts reminds her of the way Harry taught the same subject to Dumbledore's Army.

Throughout the series, Rowling reinforces the emotional parallels between Harry and Snape. Prejudice and negativity cloud their judgment of each other. They provoke each other, know how to push the right buttons to get a reaction. "'I am not weak,'" seethes Harry (*Order of the Phoenix* 536). "'DON'T . . . CALL ME COWARD!'" yells Snape (*Half-Blood Prince* 604). In the "Occlumency" chapter of *Order of the Phoenix*, Snape rants about those who "'wear their hearts proudly on their sleeves,'" "'wallow in sad memories,'" and are unable to master their emotions (536). This applies to Harry, the broody, angry fifteen-year-old, but it also applies to Snape himself, still carrying around the hurts and grudges of his youth.

Why does Rowling only allow Harry to glimpse Snape's memories of childhood unhappiness (and possible abuse) and adolescent loneliness and humiliation? Where are the adult memories? One reason for this is that Rowling is using Snape to make a point about the lasting effects of bullying. Children who are bullied, as Snape was, often grow up to be bullies, as we can see from Snape's torment of Harry, the son of his tormentor. But there's another reason Rowling only shows Harry (and us) these particular memories of Snape's: she is reinforcing the idea that Snape is emotionally stuck in adolescence. Look at the dominant personality traits Rowling has given Snape. He is angry, jealous, paranoid, self-pitying, and insecure; he is unable to control his temper, and thinks he knows everything. In short, Snape is an overgrown teenager. And this neatly parallels the teenage angst Harry is feeling himself.

Rowling uses Dumbledore, her figure of wisdom and benevolent authority, to underscore (and validate) the emotional connection between Snape and Harry, these two immature, unfinished boys. Dumbledore is the one who pushes them together for Occlumency lessons, like a father trying to get his squabbling sons to be nice to each other. Remember also that Dumbledore is sitting on the missing information about why he trusts Snape. As we speculated earlier, it involves Snape's relationship with Lily. If that speculation is correct, then Snape and Harry are also connected through their feelings for Lily. And because Lily is associated with maternal love, this creates the image of Snape and Harry as some sort of unwitting spiritual brothers—an interesting storytelling choice, wouldn't you say?

Rowling links Snape and Harry further through Dumbledore by having him ask each of them seperately to carry out a task so disagreeable that both initially refuse. In the forest argument overheard by Hagrid, Snape tells Dumbledore he no longer wants to do something he agreed to do, but Dumbledore doesn't let him off the hook. In the cave, Harry hesitates when Dumbledore asks for his word that he will do everything in his power to make him keep drinking the potion. Just as he does with Snape, Dumbledore reminds Harry that they have an agreement (earlier, Dumbledore made Harry swear to follow any command he might give him before allowing him to come along on the search for the Horcrux). What could Rowling be telling us, but not telling us, here? That if Dumbledore could order Harry to make him drink poison and, in effect, kill him, it is just as likely that Dumbledore could order Snape to perform a similar deed?

Finally, we come to a stunning parallel that suggests that Snape and Harry are on the same side. Rowling uses nearly identical wording to describe Harry and Snape's reactions as they obey Dumbledore's commands. On page 571 of *Half-Blood Prince*, as Harry is forcing Dumbledore to drink the poison, Rowling describes Harry as, "Hating himself, repulsed by what he was doing." On page 595, just before Snape levels the *Avada Kedavra*, Rowling tells us that "Snape gazed for a moment at Dumbledore, and there was revulsion and hatred etched in the harsh lines of his face." The similarity in the wording almost leaps off the pages. But there is a difference, too. With Harry, she is telling us that the hate he was feeling was directed at himself; with Snape, she tells us only of the appearance of hate on his face, not at whom it was directed. Ambiguity, always ambiguity.

However, there could be a subtle indication of Snape's loyalty in her wording. By telling us what Harry is feeling first, it's as if she means us to take that explanation as a guide to how we might interpret the "revulsion and hatred" on Snape's face. Either Snape hates himself, or he hates Dumbledore at that moment for making him do it. Those who are inclined to take Snape's look of hatred at face value should, at the very least, remember the first rule of reading Rowling: Things are not always what they seem. And remember, also, that we are watching the killing of Dumbledore through Harry's eyes, which are under three layers of veiling at the time: glasses, the Invisibility Cloak, and darkness. As we discussed in the "Looks Can Be Deceiving" section, that's triple the metaphor for misunderstanding.

## Snape's Redemptive Path

As Rowling has repeatedly shown us, Harry and Snape are both immature. They both need to grow up in order for their journeys to be complete. Harry needs to learn that looks can be deceiving; he must learn to stop pre-judging and popping off based on emotion, learn to be patient, to interpret things correctly, to see, to understand. He also has to get past the desire for vengeance against Snape, because this is a distraction from the noble task at hand, fighting the good fight against Voldemort. And if Harry cannot master his hatred of Snape, he risks becoming just like him, emotionally stunted and bitter.

As for Snape, he will only be able to grow up when he puts the past behind him and stops shadowboxing with James Potter. Snape wants more than anything to prove he is not a coward—specifically he wants to prove it to James, through Harry. He will never get the respect he wants until he learns to stop wallowing in the past. Also, if he is genuinely remorseful, Snape has to confess this to Harry, no matter how distasteful Snape finds the idea of wearing his heart on his sleeve. He has to deal with his adult emotions for once, in order to truly atone for the death of Lily and James. Harry's acknowledgment of Snape's courage is the only thing that can free Snape from the emotional scars James inflicted on him. And Harry is the only one who can forgive Snape for his part in Lily's death. Rowling has bonded Snape and Harry as tightly as any Unbreakable Vow could. Harry is the key to Snape's redemption.

How do we know Snape is on the path to redemption? Rowling hinted so herself in a 1999 radio interview with the Boston WBUR "The Connection" radio program, when she was read a listener's question about Snape's "redemptive pattern." Well, okay—she didn't hint so much as dance around the question, nervously. This was Rowling's answer in its entirety: "He, um. . . . There's so much I wish I could say to you, and I can't because it would ruin. . . . I promise you, whoever asked that question, can I just say to you that I'm slightly stunned that you've said that and you'll find out why I'm so stunned if you read Book Seven. That's all I'm going to say."

Besides that intriguing statement, there is, as we noted earlier, the following Potterverse evidence that Snape could be working toward redemption: Dumbledore's belief in his remorse and trust in his loyalty, his work as a spy for Dumbledore and his efforts to protect Harry. There is also compelling evidence that Snape is on a journey of redemption in the emotional baggage with which Rowling has burdened him. Shame is a constant theme in Snape's life (made worse because of his hyper-sensitive ego). In *Order of the Phoenix*, we are given glimpses of Snape's childhood, and for the first time in the series it is possible for us (as well as Harry) to feel sorry for him. In one such glimpse, the young Snape cries as his father—a Muggle—appears to be threatening his cowering mother. Was his father also violent toward him? Did he use shame as a weapon? Later in the Pensieve scene, Snape is subjected by James to the shame of being hung upside down in front of their classmates to reveal his shabby, unwashed underpants; he has never recovered from the humiliation of James getting the better of him.

The litany of shame continues: he is unpopular; he is ugly; he had to be rescued from a werewolf by the popular, loathesome James. Snape is ashamed of being a half-blood and gives himself a royal-sounding title. If the theory of his friendship with Lily is true, then imagine the shame and guilt he feels over her death. Like an addict forced into rehab, he is not allowed to teach Defense Against the Dark Arts because he might relapse—more shame. By the end of *Half-Blood Prince*, he is hated as a betrayer and a traitor. How much shame can one person endure—how much does one person deserve? When we see a character suffer so relentlessly, we begin to wonder if perhaps it's all a build-up to some relief down the road. Is Rowling putting Snape through hell now because she wants us to feel later on that he has earned his state of grace? Not that a state of grace for Snape will necessarily mean living happily ever after. In the end, Rowling may give him what he most wants in the world—he will prove that he is not a coward—but he will still have to answer for the death of James and Lily (not to mention Dumbledore). As a Shapeshifter, his journey has to end with a final, unambiguous action—like dying a hero—in order to prove his commitment to the side of good.

Finally, the theory that Snape is on a redemptive path is strongly supported by the powerful scene from the *Harry Potter and the Prisoner of Azkaban* movie in which Snape throws himself in front of Harry, Ron, and Hermione as the werewolf Lupin advances on them. This image of a courageous Snape protecting Harry while confronting one of the traumas of his own past is unforgettable; it far overshadows the film's scenes of Snape being sinister. The fact that this scene was invented by the screenwriter, with Rowling's approval, raises many questions. Why allow such a balance-tilting scene to remain in the film? Is this a foreshadowing of (shapeshifting) events to come? Is it a hint of Snape's allegiance to Dumbledore?

Any speculation about Snape's possible redemption assumes that he is either on Dumbledore's side or Voldemort's. But there is a third possibility which we haven't yet discussed. Snape could be neither white nor black, but gray. He could be a mercenary whose only concerns are furthering his own agenda and saving his own skin. Rowling has given us much cause to take this view of a slippery Snape willing to pledge allegiance to whichever flag is flying higher. (The idea of a mercenary Snape could well explain why he stayed put at Hogwarts all those years after Voldemort's fall.) Snape is ambitious; Rowling shows us this in *Sorcerer's Stone* in the first Potions class scene, when he rapturously tells the class that he can teach them to "'bottle fame, brew glory, even stopper death'" (137). Fame, glory, immortality—these are Snape's dreams, outwardly at least. Snape could simply be willing to follow the leader most likely to help him get what he wants. Snape could turn out to be the Gollum figure of the story, helping the hero defeat the enemy not because he intends to, but because he succumbs to his own selfish desires. But, while a Snape who is only looking out for himself is a plausible scenario, it's not as dramatic or as emotionally satisfying a payoff as having him take a stand and declare a loyalty. This is just intuition, mind you. But it feels like Rowling has spent all this effort wrapping Snape in ambiguity for one reason: to have him cast it off and surprise us all, one way or another, in the final act.

Harry will almost certainly have the opportunity to kill Snape at some point in Book Seven—the dramatic and emotional resolution of the saga demands that they meet again. And Snape and Harry still have to learn the lessons they can only learn from each other. Let's say that Harry kills Snape. What does Snape learn from that? Well, yes, he learns not to mess with Harry, but does it resolve any of the issues Snape needs to resolve in order to complete his journey? No. And does killing Snape help Harry to grow up? No, it merely allows him to gratify his taste for revenge. Wouldn't it be a much richer story if Harry has Snape at his mercy, and uses it? Snape is apparently the only person left who holds the missing information about why Dumbledore trusted him. And he is the only person who can tell us what was going on between him and Dumbledore the night Dumbledore was killed. But, as it stands now, Harry is unlikely to be convinced by any confession or explanation from Severus Snape. Something drastic needs to happen in order for Harry to believe him.

Think back to Rowling's many references to Harry having his mother's eyes. What if Harry has indeed inherited Lily's gift of seeing the truth of people's hearts or souls, and it manifests itself just as Harry is preparing to take his revenge on Snape? What if this is the manner in which the Shapeshifter Snape reveals his loyalty to Harry? We theorized before that Harry will need to be mature enough to believe Snape's confession when the time comes. Maybe Harry's maturity will arrive wrapped in the metaphor of "seeing" the way Lily saw, of fully understanding what's in front of him for the first time in his life. Maybe this is how Harry (and readers) will find out the truth about Snape's loyalty to Dumbledore, and accept him without doubt as being on Harry's side. Maybe this is how Harry will learn to forgive. And maybe this is how Snape will get his last chance to prove his worth. Without each other, Harry and Snape cannot

## Top Ten Reasons Why We Love Snape

1. Valiantly throws himself in front of Harry, Ron, and Hermione as the werewolf Lupin approaches them in the film version of *Prisoner of Azkaban*. The moment is made even more dramatic by a swooping camera that rushes right at Snape's anxious face from the werewolf's perspective. This heroic scene is not in the book, but J. K. Rowling approved it. Read into that what you will.

2. Counteracts Professor Quirrell's spell to knock Harry off his broom during a Quidditch match in *Sorcerer's Stone*. Gets set on fire in appreciation.

3. Smoothly deflects Dolores Umbridge's demand for Veritaserum with which she intends to interrogate Harry in *Order of the Phoenix*. "'It takes a full moon cycle to mature, so I should have it ready for you in around a month,'" he tells her (744). A hilarious example of Snape's subtle sarcasm, as well as his skill at outwitting adversaries by putting on a façade of innocence. Umbridge, you've been owned.

4. Makes an unforgettable impression in his first speech to Harry's Potions class in *Sorcerer's Stone*, hypnotically extolling "'the beauty of the softly simmering cauldron with its shimmering fumes, the delicate power of liquids that creep through human veins, bewitching the mind, ensnaring the senses'" (137). The only way this could have been a greater entrance was if Snape recited the speech while being lowered into the classroom on a harness like Tom Cruise in *Mission: Impossible*.

5. Knocks the preening Gilderoy Lockhart on his conceited butt with an unfriendly spell during a dueling demonstration in *Chamber of Secrets*. For once, we're glad Snape has a mean streak.

## Top Ten Reasons Why We Love Snape (Con't.)

6. Despite lingering animosity over their adolescent skirmishes, he dutifully supplies Professor Lupin with Wolfsbane potion to minimize the effects of his monthly transformation in *Prisoner of Azkaban*. If Snape ever marketed his potion to women, he'd be a galleonaire.

7. Looking "slightly paler than usual," he goes off to rejoin the resurrected Voldemort as Dumbledore's spy at the end of *Goblet of Fire* (713). This is our first glimpse of Snape's courageous and heroic possibilities. We can only guess at the warm welcome he receives from Voldemort. Pizza and Cruciatus, anyone?

8. Tells Dumbledore that he feels remorse for his part in the death of James and Lily Potter. Some other things Snape feels bad about: spiking McGonagall's pumpkin juice at the staff Yule party; putting fake disabled parking tags on his broom; convincing Dumbledore to deposit all his money into a Nigerian bank account.

9. "[M]uttering an incantation that sound[s] almost like song," he heals Draco after Harry badly injures him with the *Sectumsempra* spell in *Half-Blood Prince* (523). After *Half-Blood Prince*, Snape left Hogwarts to pursue a full-time career in healing. He can now be seen on the TV series *Grey's Anatomy*, where he goes by the name "Dr. McGreasy."

10. Protects Harry one last time when he saves him from being finished off by Death Eaters at the climax of *Half-Blood Prince*, cleverly reminding them that the Dark Lord wants Potter for himself. In return, Harry calls him a coward. Ungrateful punk.

vanquish the demons—both literal and personal—that prevent them both from truly becoming adults.

### And the Final Evidence That Snape Is on Harry's Side . . .

Dumbledore is Rowling's personification of wisdom, her great mentor figure in the tradition of Gandalf and Obi-Wan Kenobi. Rowling associates Dumbledore with two important lessons: that love is the greatest power in the universe, and that people deserve a chance to show that they can do the right thing. If Snape turns out to have been loyal to Voldemort all along, then Rowling leaves us with the impression that Dumbledore was weak and gullible. Worse, she negates what Dumbledore stood for; the message of the saga becomes that love, forgiveness, and understanding are not stronger than hate, selfishness, and prejudice.

Would Rowling really allow Dumbledore to languish under this cloud for all time? His reputation must be redeemed in Book Seven. Only by making Snape loyal to Dumbledore and by having Harry (and readers) fully see and understand the reasons for Dumbledore's trust, can Rowling restore our faith in Dumbledore's wisdom. Yes, making Snape the villain he outwardly seems would be a valid storytelling choice, but it seems an easier road than Rowling has thus far taken. As Dumbledore says in *Goblet of Fire*, we all have to make a choice between doing what is right and doing what is easy. In making Severus Snape a good guy despite all appearances, Rowling will be doing what is right.

# II.
# SNAPE THE HERO

# THE GREAT SNAPE DEBATE

IT'S ALL ABOUT THE UNDERPANTS.

Throughout the first four books of the Harry Potter series, J. K. Rowling paints a picture of Severus Snape as a dark, menacing figure who glides around Hogwarts with his black robes "rippling in a cold breeze" (*Chamber of Secrets* 78) and icy sarcasm frosting his lips. Snape is not so much a person as a walking storm cloud. But then, in *Order of the Phoenix*, Rowling does the unexpected thing and makes him human. She shows us Snape's worst memory, and it's something many of us have nightmares about: being caught in public in our underwear. And not our best underwear, either.

As Harry sneaks a peek at Snape's thoughts in the Pensieve, he sees a teenaged "Snivellus" being teased and bullied by Harry's father, James. Compared to the popular, handsome James and his easygoing pals Sirius Black and Remus Lupin, Snape stands apart as a "round-shouldered" kid with a "stringy, pallid look about him." Snape's hair is "lank and greasy"; he walks in a "twitchy manner" that Rowling compares to a spider. He arrived at Hogwarts knowing more about the Dark Arts than anyone else, and in the Pensieve, we see him hunched over his Defense Against the Dark Arts O.W.L. test, absorbed in filling scroll after scroll with his small, cramped handwriting. A few moments later, as James begins picking on him, a crowd of students gathers to watch appreciatively. "Snape was clearly unpopular," Rowling writes (640–646).

Observing Snape in this scene, we feel that we know exactly the kind of kid he must have been. If he attended a typical Muggle high school today, he'd be the black-clad Goth with the eyeliner and the multiple piercings, the one who freaks the more conservative kids out. Maybe there are rumors around school that he worships the devil. Maybe it's hard to have a conversation with him (if anyone even tries), because he's so sarcastic and acts so superior and it's hard to even understand what he's talking about. And he has this spooky way of looking right into your eyes, like he's reading your mind.

So maybe this kid—Severus—is weird and creepy. But does he deserve to be bullied the way James Potter bullies him? James uses a *Levicorpus* spell to hang Severus upside down in front of their classmates, who laugh as gravity tugs on Severus's robes to reveal his "graying"—as in dirty—underpants. How would you feel if you were Snape in this situation, hanging helplessly in front of—oh, no—Lily Evans, the pretty girl from your Potions class, while James threatens to make your underpants disappear? How long do you think it would take you to get over this complete and devastating humiliation?

In *Order of the Phoenix*, Snape is transformed from an almost cartoonishly shifty antagonist into a complex, emotionally damaged person, unable to get past the pain of his adolescence. Even Harry (briefly) feels sympathy for him, especially when he penetrates Snape's mind during an Occlumency lesson and glimpses further disturbing memories of Snape as a lonely and possibly abused child. Snape's unhappy, traumatized youth explains (although not excuses) his adult coldness and the glee with which he torments Harry.

After we learn all this about Snape, it colors everything else that we know about him—or, because Rowling makes him so enigmatic, everything we *think* we know about him. The underpants, and the shame they represent, are at the root of everything. It's easy to imagine that Snape's humiliation at the hands of James Potter made him even more eager to join the Death Eaters—it would be a way to gain power, respect, revenge. Maybe Dumbledore was the only adult who ever showed him kindness; maybe this is why Snape turns spy for him against Lord Voldemort, and why Snape maintains his loyalty even when it means obeying the most difficult order Dumbledore gives him.

Rather than unequivocally establishing him as a bad guy, Snape's killing of Dumbledore in *Half-Blood Prince* has had the opposite effect on many readers. To these fans, Snape has become a tragic hero who carries out the killing on Dumbledore's command. Perhaps, they suggest, it was part of a plan to protect Snape's cover within Voldemort's camp and position himself as an ally for Harry in his final showdown with the Dark Lord. Yes, Snape has personality issues; he's arrogant and bitter and his social skills haven't improved since high school. But Dumbledore still judged him to be trustworthy. And this darkly heroic Snape has been working on Dumbledore's behalf all along, putting his life on the line to help Harry, even though the blasted, stubborn boy refuses to see it. At the end of *Half-Blood Prince*, Snape stands alone, hated and misunderstood; to Harry, as well as to Snape's former colleagues at Hogwarts and fellow members of Dumbledore's Order of the Phoenix, he is a traitor and a murderer.

The idea of Snape as a good guy in bad guy's clothes (and with a bad guy's temperament) comes from a long tradition of anti-heroes in literature and pop culture. The anti-hero stands in contrast to the traditional hero, whose motives are clear-cut and pure and who uses honorable means to achieve his ends. Instead, the anti-hero hero, such as Shakespeare's Hamlet, may set out to right a wrong, but he lets some weakness in his character, or some doubts about his ability to do good, lead him astray. He is frequently dark-haired or swarthy. He can be an outcast, or a rebel trying to make a stand against a narrow-minded society. Or, in Snape's case, he can be a deeply flawed person trying to redeem himself. The anti-hero carries within him villainous characteristics: past sins, selfish motives, a tendency toward brutality. Indeed, he's closer to being the bad guy than the good guy.

## Sympathy for the Devil

*The Norton Anthology of English Literature* traces the literary roots of the anti-hero to the portrayal of Satan in John Milton's *Paradise Lost* (1667), an epic retelling of the Biblical story of Adam and Eve. Although he is clearly the villain of the piece, Milton's Satan is strangely heroic in his rebellion against what he believes is the tyranny of God. He is impressively intelligent and courageous in the first sections of the poem, but in later sections, his monumental pride and his overpowering need for vengeance are his undoing.

Later, in literature's Romantic era, the poet Lord Byron was partially influenced by Milton's Satan in creating the fatally flawed heroes of his epics "Childe Harolde's Pilgrimage" (1812–1818), and "The Corsair" and "Lara" (both 1814). The Byronic hero (this term refers to the poet's protagonists, as well as to the larger-than-life Byron himself, who was the equivalent of a rock star in his day) rejects conventional society. He is often the victim of uncontrollable pride and other self-destructive emotions and passions. He is haunted by some deep-rooted shame or secret crime. Three decades later, the Brontë sisters created two of the greatest and most enduring Byronic heroes in literature, the stern, dark-browed Edward Rochester in Charlotte's *Jane Eyre* (1846) and the "gipsy" Heathcliff in Emily's *Wuthering Heights* (1847). Both Rochester and Heathcliff are loners who nurse deep emotional wounds and dark secrets; they carry an aura of mystery and violent passions about them.

J. K. Rowling has endowed Snape with traces of all his anti-hero ancestors. Like Satan, Snape has a superior intellect, but is consumed by pride and the desire for revenge. Like Byron's heroes, Snape wishes to do good, but he is susceptible to self-destructive patterns and emotions (his hatred of James). Like Heathcliff, who lashes out at his romantic rival Edgar Linton by marrying and mistreating his sister and forcing Linton's daughter into servitude, Snape cruelly takes revenge on the relative (Harry) of his rival. Snape and Heathcliff are also both obsessed with pursuing the respect out of which they feel they have been cheated, and they share the dark features that mark them as persons to be feared by conventional society. And like Rochester, who is consumed with guilt over a mad wife hidden away in a secret room, Snape is emotionally and psychologically haunted by guilt and remorse over the death of Lily, with whom he possibly had a friendship, and James.

Besides Snape, Dr. Gregory House from the TV series *House* is probably the best-known current example of a Brontë-style anti-hero. House and Snape share many personality traits. They are both egotists, but both have earned the right to be full of themselves, because they are brilliant at what they do—House solves impossible medical mysteries, Snape is an exemplary Potions Master (if you ignore the fact that he seems to hate kids). Obviously, neither Snape nor House are people persons; they are sarcastic, arrogant, and angry. Like Snape, House is the meanest teacher in the school, bullying and humiliating his staff of young doctors. Both House and Snape are emotionally damaged (as a bonus, House is also physically damaged—he has a bad leg and walks with a cane). And both are really into Potions. Well, House is into one potion in particular—he has an addiction to painkillers.

Snape and House have joined an elite group of anti-heroes over whom female readers have swooned for years, including Heathcliff and Rochester and the not tragic, but still difficult, anti-hero of Jane Austen's *Pride and Prejudice*, Mr. Darcy. Blame it on the bad-boy syndrome. Anti-heroes are a challenge; they present a hard shell of coldness and disdainfulness to the world but, inside, they're vulnerable, lost boys. And whether or not it's the smart thing to do, a lot of women fall for the fantasy of breaking through the damaged anti-hero's devilish defenses to heal the wounded angel within—the way the plain little governess Jane Eyre heals her employer Rochester. On TV, House once extolled the power of his damaged leg in attracting women who felt sorry for him. Brandishing his cane, he crowed, "Chicks dig this. It's better than a puppy!" ("Detox," 1-11), and he was only half-joking. In Snape's case, substitute the graying under-

# Speculations

## Why Was Snape Wearing Graying Underpants?

What's worse than being pantsed in front of your classmates? Being pantsed in front of your classmates while wearing dingy underwear. Snape experiences this life-scarring humiliation as a teenager at Hogwarts. James Potter turns him upside down with a *Levicorpus* spell, causing his robes to fall upward and display his "graying underpants" to the laughing throng.

This scene from *Order of the Phoenix* is the first one in the books to cast Snape in a sympathetic role. And a lot of its pathos comes from those graying underpants. What does their shabby state tell us about Snape? Well, white underpants turn gray over time from repeated washings, so his underpants were not new. We know from glimpses of his memories in *Order of the Phoenix* that he was a scraggly, skinny (malnourished?) child and his father appears to have been abusive to him and his mother. In *Half-Blood Prince*, we learn that Snape's father was a Muggle. It's possible that the Snapes were not financially well off; perhaps Snape's father left the family, or rejected his son when he displayed wizarding powers (we're told that Snape arrived at Hogwarts with an unusual knowledge of Dark magic, so Snape must have shown his aptitude at an early age). Maybe Snape was attending Hogwarts on a scholarship because of financial hardship, and his mother simply had no money to give Snape for incidentals like new underwear.

Then again, in the humiliation scene, the teenage Snape is portrayed as greasy and unkempt and completely absorbed in his Defense Against the Dark Arts O.W.L. test. He wanders out of the test oblivious to his surroundings, poring over an exam paper. Snape is clearly the type of kid who is off in his own world, probably wrapped up in his extracurricular experiments into the Dark Arts—the wizarding equivalent of (really violent) video games. His head is simply not into remembering unimportant things like eating, showering, and changing his underwear.

Even Severus Snape was once a typical teenage boy.

pants for the cane; they're a symbol of Snape's vulnerability, the perceived emotional wound that needs to be healed.

While it's true that many female fans are enthralled by these misunderstood heroes, don't get the wrong impression—male characters don't have a monopoly on anti-hero qualities. There are misunderstood heroines, too, women with dark pasts, emotional scars, strong ambitions, and bad reputations. The list includes Faith from the TV series *Buffy the Vampire Slayer*; Kate on TV's *Lost*; Catwoman in the Batman comics, graphic novels, TV series, and the movie *Batman Returns* (but not the Halle Berry movie); and the greatest anti-heroine of all time, Scarlett O'Hara in *Gone with the Wind*. Snape has much in common with at least one of these misunderstood heroines—Elphaba, the Wicked Witch of the West, whose pre-*Wizard of Oz* story is sympathetically told in the book and Broadway musical *Wicked*. Snape and Elphaba are both outcasts (he's greasy, she's green) whose fierce intelligence and pride are their greatest strengths and their biggest flaws. Hey, Snape and Elphaba even dress alike!

### Knockin' on Heaven's Door

Han Solo in Star Wars is another anti-hero whose story may tell us where Snape is headed. Solo is a vivid example of a type of character called the Shapeshifter. The Shapeshifter, as we discussed in "In Defense of Snape," "serves the dramatic function of bringing doubt and suspense into the story" (Vogler 67). The Shapeshifter can start out as good, bad, or neutral, but always switches sides at a crucial point in the story; the hero often isn't sure of his loyalty until the last minute. In *Star Wars*, the mercenary Solo deserts Luke rather than take part in what he calls a "suicide mission" to protect the Rebel base. But then, he surprisingly reveals a compassionate heart hidden beneath his cynical exterior when he returns in the Millennium Falcon just in time to aid Luke in his climactic aerial battle with Darth Vader. It isn't hard to imagine Snape making a similarly dramatic last-minute statement. After all, Rowling has worked so hard to keep Snape's true loyalty in doubt that even though she has shown him killing Dumbledore, many fans still don't believe what they've witnessed. They refuse to write Snape off as a bad guy; they're certain that a misunderstood hero is waiting in the wings while Rowling sets up a bombshell of a plot twist that will prove his innocence once and for all.

Anti-heroes who shift from bad to good are often also the ones who achieve some measure of redemption through their unexpected heroism. Many readers who believe in Snape's innocence also believe that Snape is on a redemptive path. But he can only atone for his past sins (specifically, for providing Voldemort with the information that leads to Lily and James's death) by proving that he is on Harry's side and helping him defeat Voldemort in the final battle. Two well-known Shapeshifters and anti-heroes whose tragic fate might foreshadow Snape's own are Sydney Carton, who shifts from neutral to good in Charles Dickens's classic novel *A Tale of Two Cities,* and Spike, the vampire with a soul, who shifts from bad to good in *Buffy the Vampire Slayer.*

Throughout much of *A Tale of Two Cities,* which is set during the French Revolution, Carton, an English lawyer living in Paris, is an apathetic and melancholy figure. He has lived a self-destructive and slothful life. Then he falls in love with the virtuous Lucie Manette, who marries his friend, the aristocrat Charles Darnay. When Darnay is condemned to die on the guillotine and Carton overhears plans for the arrest of Lucie and her father as well, the Englishman takes heroic action that saves the woman he loves and her family. On *Buffy the Vampire Slayer,* Spike begins as Buffy's bloodsucking enemy but they become unlikely allies against bigger bads; their relationship eventually turns romantic, and even after they break up, Spike remains devoted to Buffy and her cause. He sees her as a beacon of goodness and healing, much the same way Carton sees Lucie—and as we've theorized in "In Defense of Snape"—Snape saw Lily.

There are some interesting similarities between Snape and Spike. Both have been bad boys (Death Eater, say hello to vampire), but both have sympathizing shame in their pasts. Before becoming a vampire, Spike was a wimpy Victorian poet scorned by the woman he loved. The equivalent of graying underpants in Spike's story is an ineptly written poem that he recites for his love, only to be humiliated and ridiculed for it by her "proper" society friends. And while Snape and Spike both feel remorse for the havoc they wreaked during their time on the dark side, they hide the guilt behind sword-sharp sarcasm.

These sympathizing shames may make the anti-hero's past sins understandable, but tragically, these sins still make him ineligible for a happy ending. Redemption usually demands a steep price. Heathcliff becomes obsessed with the ghost of his dead love until he finally dies alone on the moor. Rochester is scarred and blinded. Spike goes to his death help-ing Buffy save the world. Carton springs Darnay from prison and sacri-fices his own life by taking Darnay's place on the scaffold: "It is a far, far better thing that I do, than I have ever done; it is a far, far better rest that I go to, than I have ever known" (390). Is Snape capable of making such a sacrifice? Could he save Harry by revealing himself as an ally at the last moment, and go down in a blaze of glory at the hands of a Death Eater or Voldemort himself? The answer is yes. Snape is a deep pool of anti-heroism waiting to be tapped.

Those who believe that Snape is the Judas he appears to be and did indeed betray Dumbledore have to consider the fact that even Judas has his supporters these days. Evidence that Judas, the most famous Shapeshifter in history, might have been an anti-hero rather than a vil-lain surfaced recently with the discovery of an ancient Egyptian Christian text called the Gospel of Judas. Published in *National Geographic* in May 2006, the text, dating from the third or fourth centu-ry A.D., states that Judas betrayed Jesus on Jesus' orders. Writing about the discovery, blogcritics.org commentator Eric Olsen wondered if the final Harry Potter book will reveal "The Gospel of Snape."

## A Hero Will Rise

The idea of Snape as a hero is irresistible. He is so cruel, so intimidating, so enigmatic—and yet, there is such potential within him to do good. We see this in the way he protects and teaches Harry, even though he apparently loathes him. And we see it in Dumbledore's trust in his remorse and loyalty. We are attracted to Snape the anti-hero because we love the idea of a fallen angel redeemed, of someone finding the courage or compassion to do the right thing no matter what the cost. We love the idea of the misfit, the outcast, the loser, who suddenly stands up and shows the world that he is better, stronger, and braver than anyone thought he could be. We love the idea of transformation. And what is the Harry Potter saga about, if not transformation? The unloved orphan is really a wizard; the ordinary world is really a place of hidden magic. And the bad guy is really a good guy.

The deeper into the pit of sin, cruelty, and despair the misunderstood hero falls, the riper he is for transformation, and the greater that trans-formation will be. The anti-hero is so fascinating because, unlike the traditional hero, he has to make the conscious choice to be good. And while that impulse might be in his nature, it has been buried so deeply by life's blows and his own bad habits that he's not even sure it's still there. But when he makes that choice, he does so knowing it will cost him dearly—more dearly, even, than it will cost the hero. Anti-heroes give us the best of both worlds: we get the thrill of following them into darkness, yet we are moved when they reach toward the light.

Snape has all the necessary elements to be considered one of the greatest of all literary anti-heroes. He is classically sinister, yet those graying underpants give him away. How much will you wager that the trauma of being so cruelly exposed in adolescence is the reason Snape adopted the severely buttoned-up uniform of his adulthood? He was determined that nobody would ever see his underpants again. Nobody would ever hurt him or know what he was feeling or thinking. But Snape fools himself. In protecting Harry and in (we hope) pledging allegiance to Dumbledore, Snape has shown us his most naked yearning: like all misunderstood characters, Snape just wants to be understood.

# III.
# THE LIFE OF SEVERUS SNAPE: MALIGNED AND MISUNDERSTOOD

SEVERUS SNAPE, UNSUNG HERO in the fight against Voldemort, was born on January 9 in 1958, 1959, or 1960, making him a Capricorn. People who are born under this sign are said to be "hardworking, unemotional, shrewd, practical, responsible, persevering, and cautious to the extreme . . . capable of persisting for as long as is necessary to accomplish a goal they have set for themselves. They are reliable workers in almost any profession they undertake. They are the major finishers of most projects started by the 'pioneering' signs; with firm stick-to-it-ness they quickly become the backbone of any company they work for. . . . They strive always for honesty in their criticism of self, they respect discipline from above and demand it from those beneath them. In their methodical, tough, stubborn, unyielding way, they persist against personal hardship, putting their families and/or their work before their own needs and welfare to reach their objectives long after others have given up and fallen by the wayside" (Astrology Online).

Little is known about his parents or whether they are still alive. His mother Eileen Prince was a pure-blooded witch who once was the captain of the Gobstones Team at Hogwarts. His father Tobias Snape, a man who possessed no wizard blood, was hot-tempered, overbearing, and possibly abusive to his wife and young son. The young Severus, growing up in their household and forced to witness their arguments, as a result became a lonely, insecure child who, to take his mind off his circumstances, developed unhealthy magic interests before he understood their danger.

Based on dates and ages found in the Harry Potter series, we can estimate that Snape attended Hogwarts School of Witchcraft and Wizardry at some point between the years 1969 and 1978. An exceptionally talented first-year student, his skills in some areas eclipsed even seventh-year students despite his lack of formal training. Although his natural intelligence and courage could have just as easily landed him in Ravenclaw or Gryffindor, his pragmatic nature and early magic usage caused the Sorting Hat to sort him into Slytherin. His House affiliation led him to encounters with fellow Slytherins and future Death Eaters Lucius Malfoy and Bellatrix Black, older students who likely provided the first measure of acceptance he'd ever received. However, as a half-blood, he would have remained an object of contempt by the pure-blooded members of Slytherin who surrounded him. Snape struggled to fit in, although he still lacked the social skills to do so easily.

# The Case for Snape's Innocence

James Potter, Lily Evans, Sirius Black, Remus Lupin, and Peter Pettigrew—all members of Gryffindor House—entered Hogwarts the same year as Snape, but the teenage Snape was unpopular and isolated and had trouble making friends his own age. He suffered relentless bullying at the hands of the Marauders, a gang of Gryffindor students of which James Potter was the ringleader. The Marauders teased poor Snape unmercifully, taunting him at every turn: "'What're you going to do, Snivelly, wipe your nose on us?'" (*Order of the Phoenix* 646). Despite strong innate skills at magic, Snape simply didn't *look* as if he belonged; his appearance and social awkwardness ostracized him and made him an easy target for bullying. Snape appeared to have a "stringy, pallid look about him, like a plant kept in the dark. His hair was lank and greasy and was flopping onto the table, his hooked nose barely half an inch from the surface of the parchment as he scribbled" (*Order of the Phoenix* 640–641).

A natural at brewing potions, Snape was able to improve on many of the standard potion recipes taught at Hogwarts. He recorded these improvements in his textbook, later discovered by Harry, who used Snape's scribbled notes to, among other things, save Ron's life. We know from the inside cover of this textbook that, during his school days, Snape referred to himself as "the Half-Blood Prince," a clever yet self-depreciating reference to his half-Muggle bloodline as well as his mother's magical lineage.

By the end of his fifth year, the Marauders' bullying had come to a head: unprovoked, and using Snape's own spell (a spell that Harry found scrawled in the margins of Snape's old Potions text years later) against him, James hung him upside down in mid-air so that his underwear showed. (When Lily, defending Snape, asked James why he had done that to him, James answered, "'Well . . . it's more the fact that he *exists*, if you know what I mean . . .'" [*Order of the Phoenix* 647].) Disarmed, Snape was humiliated and outnumbered, but showed remarkable courage as he used nothing more than words to strike back at his tormentors—courage that presaged the strength of character he would later demonstrate in the fight against Voldemort.

Lily Evans, it must be noted, stood up for Snape when James and Sirius hexed him, declaring how much she hated her future husband. Snape repaid her by calling her "'Mudblood,'" but the insult was just the lashing out of an angry, embarrassed boy without any other defense; he came from Muggle blood just as she did. Evidence points to the possibility of Lily and Snape having shared a bond at some point, perhaps even a friendship; Lily's talent in Potions was apparently equal to Snape's, which could have been due either to similar talents or to Snape helping her in the subject. In either case, it is clear Lily did not hate Snape the way James and the others did.

And they did indeed hate the young Snape, tormenting the outsider at every turn, and the worst of the Marauders' dirty tricks nearly cost Snape his life. Trying to scare Snape, Sirius tricked him into following Lupin through a passage beneath the Whomping Willow that grows on Hogwarts's grounds, planning for Snape to encounter a vicious werewolf—Lupin's lupine form, dangerously out of control—at the Shrieking Shack at the passage's end. James, however, perhaps in the midst of a crisis of conscience that would later transform him into the upstanding member of wizarding society he eventually became, stopped Snape from going through the passage, saving his life. Had James not stopped him, Snape could very well have been killed or, at the very least, bitten and infected, becoming a werewolf himself. Snape became indebted to James because of this, although he was aware that James only knew of the plot because he had been involved, and suspected (not without reason) that James was more concerned about his own standing at Hogwarts than about Snape's safety.

Snape never reported this near-deadly prank to Dumbledore or anyone else on the Hogwarts staff, protecting the Marauders from certain punishment. Had Snape exposed them, James would have never been named Head Boy. Instead, Snape remained silent, keeping Lupin's secret to himself for years and thereby giving Lupin the opportunity to live a nearly normal life.

After leaving Hogwarts, Snape followed the example of the only group of people who had ever accepted and welcomed him: his older Slytherin Housemates. He joined the Death Eaters, becoming one of Voldemort's official followers. They branded him with the Dark Mark, an image that would continue to reappear on his arm long after he had renounced the group and its Dark ways. But it was in this group that his talents at magic, especially those he had developed as a child, were finally appreciated. It was his role within Voldemort's ranks that led him to the Hog's Head Inn on the same night as Sybill Trelawney spoke the prophecy that we now know proved to be Voldemort's downfall.

One of his missions, a mission that turned out to be one of his last as a true Death Eater, was to seek a teaching job at Hogwarts, the stronghold of Voldemort's greatest enemy, Dumbledore. It was because of these orders that Snape, still a very young man at the time, happened to be at the Inn where Dumbledore was interviewing Trelawney for the post of Divination professor. During the interview, Snape stood at the door of Trelawney's room, and so overheard part of the now-infamous prophecy she made there. Not realizing the tragic consequences to which his actions would lead, he reported what he had heard to Voldemort. His information eventually led to the Potters' betrayal at the hands of Peter Pettigrew, the murders of James and Lily Potter, the failed attack on their infant son Harry, and the (first) downfall of Voldemort himself.

Wracked with guilt once he learned how Voldemort had interpreted the words he, Snape, had reported back to him, Snape made a decision that instantly put his life at risk. He turned away from the Death Eaters and went to Dumbledore in order to stop Voldemort and his supporters, offering his services as a double agent. Dumbledore, a forgiving man capable of believing the best of others, accepted him. It was at this point that Snape became a secret member of the Order of the Phoenix, keeping Dumbledore abreast of the activities and plans of the Death Eaters. As Dumbledore told Harry:

> "Professor Snape made a terrible mistake. He was still in Lord Voldemort's employ on the night he heard the first half of Professor Trelawney's prophecy. Naturally, he hastened to tell his master what he had heard, for it concerned his master most deeply. But he did not know—he had no possible way of knowing—which boy Voldemort would hunt from then onward, or that the parents he would destroy in his murderous quest were people that Professor Snape knew, that they were your mother and father. . . . You have no idea of the remorse Professor Snape felt when he realized how Lord Voldemort had interpreted the prophecy, Harry. I believe it to be the greatest regret of his life and the reason that he returned" (*Half-Blood Prince* 549).

It was because of this regret that Dumbledore chose to trust Snape, both then and throughout the years that followed.

Dumbledore also awarded Snape a safe haven in the form of a teaching position at Hogwarts, a move that later proved helpful as it effectively fooled the Death Eaters into believing that Snape had been carrying out his original mission during Voldemort's absence. However, the teaching position was not the one that he had originally sought. Snape had hoped to teach Defense Against the Dark Arts due to his long interest in the Dark Arts, dating back to before his time at Hogwarts (before he fully understood the consequences of such studies). Knowing the true dangers of the Dark Arts as he did, as well as how easily one could be tempted into using them, he felt he would be an ideal choice. However, Dumbledore decided that another position might suit him better. We can only guess at Dumbledore's reasons, but likely explanations include a desire to alleviate some of the concern among parents who might learn — or might already have known — about his ties to Voldemort, and a need for Snape to actually remain on the Hogwarts staff: the Defense Against the Dark Arts teaching position had been cursed by Voldemort years before, and since then, no teacher had lasted more than one year.

Instead, Dumbledore offered him a position as the Hogwarts Potions Master, a job which Snape accepted as it gave him a place to belong and, more importantly, a second chance. However, still believing that his prior experience could do some good, Snape made no secret of his desire to teach Defense Against the Dark Arts and reapplied for the position yearly. He continued to work diligently for Dumbledore despite this disappointment, and despite the fact that the headmaster, for all his claims of trusting him, did not trust him enough to give him the Defense Against the Dark Arts position until his final year at the school.

Snape worked at Hogwarts for fifteen years, developing a reputation as a strict taskmaster. His strictness was necessary: Snape had only been away from Hogwarts for five years, which meant that some of the older students at the school could have remembered him as a student. Snape would have been forced to distance himself from those students as, if they remembered him, they probably remembered his many humiliations and — being children — shared the tales freely with the younger students. Under such circumstances, Snape would have been put on the defensive from the start, forcing him to adopt an aloof, callous attitude that also, it seemed, proved an effective method of teaching.

After Voldemort's first defeat, many Death Eaters were brought to trial before the Wizengamot. Snape himself was denounced as a Death Eater by Igor Karkaroff, another former Death Eater (and future headmaster of

Durmstrang) captured previous to Voldemort's defeat. Dumbledore vouched for Snape, however, and he was not charged. But outside of court, Snape clearly kept his allegiance to Dumbledore quiet, and fortunately so: soon after Voldemort's return to power in *Goblet of Fire*, the "traitor" Karkaroff was found dead, killed by the reemerged Death Eaters.

Years passed, and Snape remained at Hogwarts as Potions Master while Defense Against the Dark Arts professors cycled through yearly. Here, of course, is the point where our history may become more detailed: Harry Potter's first year at Hogwarts. The year was an eventful one, for Snape in particular. As Harry looked very much like Snape's former adversary James, Snape couldn't help but dislike the boy immediately, especially as he appeared at the school as an instant celebrity without earning the honor. However, despite his personal feelings, Snape prevented that year's Defense Against the Dark Arts instructor, Professor Quirrell, from cursing Harry's broom during a Quidditch match, thus saving his life, and later refereed the Hufflepuff/Gryffindor Quidditch match so that no one could interfere with the proceedings. This began a pattern that Harry for a long time has refused to recognize: Snape has repeatedly protected Harry's life when circumstances warranted, despite his residual hatred toward Harry's father.

Harry, not understanding Snape's attitude toward him, began to suspect Snape of wrongdoing, believing Snape to be the one who tried to curse his broomstick during a Quidditch match. After all, Snape *looked* like a villain, didn't seem like a nice guy, and was the only one that the boy could see chanting when his broomstick began to act oddly. Worse, Harry noticed that Snape had been bitten by an unknown animal shortly after an attempt had been made to get past a magical safeguard, a three-headed dog, put in place to protect the Sorcerer's Stone, and then heard him threaten Quirrell in the forest. To Harry, who didn't understand what he was seeing, these coincidences made Snape appear culpable.

Ultimately, Quirrell (and Voldemort, who Quirrell carried with him) was revealed as the true villain who sought the Sorcerer's Stone. This revelation, along with the explanations for Snape's various actions, should have cleared Snape of suspicion, especially once Harry learned that it was Snape who helped him at the Quidditch match. But despite evidence otherwise, Harry continued to suspect him no matter how many times Dumbledore stated that Snape was trustworthy.

Snape continued to teach Harry in Potions class the following year, but it was not until Harry's third year that we again received extensive details about Snape's actions. That year, Dumbledore hired Remus Lupin, werewolf and once-member of the Marauders who had bullied Snape so extensively, as the new Defense Against the Dark Arts professor. Snape had concerns—Lupin presented a danger to students, as he almost was to Snape himself—but Dumbledore disagreed with Snape's concerns, believing Lupin to be harmless as long as he consumed a potion called Wolfsbane every month—a potion Snape put aside his personal feelings in order to brew. Thanks to Snape's monthly efforts, Lupin turned into a harmless wolf instead of a ferocious killer at the full moon.

Snape substituted for Lupin in his Defense Against the Dark Arts class during the full moons and, in his very first class, the memory of his own near-miss with death due to Lupin's nature impossible to put aside, assigned an essay on how to recognize werewolves so that, should Lupin become a danger, his students would be prepared. (Only Hermione discovered Lupin's secret from that assignment, however, and she kept it to herself.) That moment came late in that year: Snape realized that the full moon was rising and Lupin had not yet taken his potion, putting everyone at the school at risk. He rushed a goblet of the potion to Lupin's office but discovered, instead of Lupin himself, the Marauder's Map, a map of the school the Marauders had created that revealed not only the secret passages around Hogwarts but also the current locations of the school's faculty and staff.

Freshly angered by finally understanding how the Marauders were able to get away with so many horrible deeds while in school but determined to get the potion to Lupin and save the students he now believed were trapped with him in the Shrieking Shack, Snape bravely retraced the steps that could have led to his death all those years ago, knowing that the same dangerous monster might lie at the end of the path. He discovered when he arrived that the situation was worse than he thought: the Shack was also the hiding place of Azkaban escapee and convicted murderer Sirius Black— the man Snape believed responsible for not only giving up the Potters' location to Voldemort but also killing the couple, Pettigrew, and twelve Muggles. (Black was also, no doubt, a harsh reminder of Snape's own guilt.)

It is worth noting, briefly, something that can be easily overlooked: when Snape entered the shack, Hermione's cat, Crookshanks (being half-Kneazle and therefore a creature that always knows a suspicious person when it sees one[1]), does not protest his arrival or any of his

---

[1] See Rowling's supplementary book *Fantastic Beasts and Where to Find Them* (officially listed as written by the fictional "Newton 'Newt' Artemis Fido Scamander"): "The Kneazle has an uncanny ability to detect unsavory or suspicious characters."

actions; the only one in the room that the cat dislikes is Scabbers the rat, even more so when transformed back into the turncoat Peter Pettigrew, the man actually responsible for betraying the Potters.

Fearing for the students' well-being and filled with residual fury at seeing two of the boys who tormented him as a teenager, Sirius and Remus, together again, Snape planned to summon the Dementors to give Sirius their "kiss" and remove his soul. After all, not only had Sirius already been sentenced to this fate by the Ministry of Magic, but Sirius was widely believed to be an extremely dangerous mass murderer, one even the Muggle authorities had been warned against. Summoning the Dementors was the only responsible course of action. But before he was able to take this appropriate action, Harry, for once better informed, immobilized Snape in order to protect his godfather Sirius. Unconscious, Snape did not learn the truth about Sirius's innocence until much later.

It's true that Snape later publicly released the information about Lupin's werewolf status to the Ministry of Magic, but Lupin had proven that he was too much of a danger to allow him to continue teaching. Lupin voluntarily resigned his position at the end of the school year, fearing that he could again become a danger to students as well, and knowing that many parents would protest his presence at Hogwarts for this very reason.

The Harry Potter series's telling of the events of the following year are largely concerned with the historic Triwizard Tournament. Snape remained Hogwarts's Potions Master (the Defense Against the Dark Arts position was filled by Alastor "Mad-Eye" Moody, who later turned out to be an imposter), but it was not until Voldemort's return that he returned to the forefront of the action. Unlike those still loyal to Voldemort, Snape was not present when Cedric Diggory was killed and Harry's blood was used to bring Voldemort back to life. However, when Voldemort returned to full life and power following the final task of the tournament, Snape's old Dark Mark reappeared on his arm, summoning him to Voldemort's side. He ignored the summons and did not rejoin the other Death Eaters in the graveyard. He instead exposed his Dark Mark to Cornelius Fudge in an attempt to help Dumbledore prove that Lord Voldemort had returned. Snape knew that preparations had to be made to fight his former master, and that they needed to begin immediately.

But that wasn't possible until they knew what Voldemort's plans were. It was then that Dumbledore asked Snape to falsely take up his former Death Eater mantle in order to infiltrate the group, and serve as a much-needed source of information.

> "Severus," said Dumbledore, turning to Snape, "you know what I must ask you to do. If you are ready . . . if you are prepared . . ."
> "I am," said Snape.
> He looked slightly paler than usual, and his cold, black eyes glittered strangely.
> "Then good luck," said Dumbledore . . . (*Goblet of Fire* 713).

As Voldemort worked to return to power, Snape risked his life as a spy inside the ranks of the Death Eaters and made regular reports to the re-formed Order of the Phoenix. Snape used his exceptional skills as an Occlumens to hide his true loyalties from his powerful former master, putting himself in jeopardy despite the fact that many in the Order remained suspicious of him.

With the real Mad-Eye Moody concentrating on the fight against Voldemort, the Defense Against the Dark Arts position was open at Hogwarts once again, but Dumbledore did not give Snape the position despite the alternative: the Ministry of Magic forcing their own choice of teacher on Hogwarts. However, Dumbledore's decision was made for good reason. It gave Snape the necessary time to concentrate on his work as a spy, a far more important task.

At first, Snape chose to appear to align himself with the new Defense Against the Dark Arts professor, Dolores Umbridge, as she, in the name of the Ministry of Magic, quickly took over Hogwarts in order to (ostensibly) protect its students. This course of action kept her, and the Ministry, away from his secret affairs, a task that became even more difficult when events forced Dumbledore out of his position. When Umbridge's investigations threatened to interfere with the work of the Order, he helped hinder her so that she would not discover too much and disrupt their plans; in one instance, he gave her fake Veritaserum when she wished to use it to question Harry as to the whereabouts of fellow Order members Dumbledore and Sirius Black (and was put on probation because of it).

At Dumbledore's request, Snape began teaching Harry Occlumency twice a week so that the boy could better protect his mind from

Voldemort and his followers, and Harry's friends and mentors supported these lessons wholeheartedly. However, overall, these lessons were disastrous, as Snape, knowing the importance of this skill, pushed Harry to exhaustion during the lessons. Making the situation even more difficult, the subject of James—a vulnerable point for both teacher and student—came up often. Snape could not control his residual resentment, and it hindered the lessons and the good they could have done for Harry. Harry himself disliked Snape too thoroughly to truly take the lessons seriously. And when Harry invaded Snape's privacy by looking at a memory Snape had stored temporarily in his Pensieve (a memory of Snape being humiliated by Harry's father), Snape ended the lessons abruptly in anger.

Though he was unable to successfully teach Harry Occlumency, he was at least able to alert the Order of the Phoenix when Harry and his friends flew to the Department of Mysteries and into Voldemort's trap. Had Snape not taken immediate action, all six of the students who went on the false rescue mission—Harry, Ron, Hermione, Neville, Luna, and Ginny—most likely would have been killed. Instead there was only one casualty: Sirius, who had rushed to his godson's aid.

Though the details were never relayed to Harry (and thus to us), we do know that, at a critical point during the summer that followed, Snape saved Dumbledore's life when the headmaster returned to Hogwarts badly injured after breaking one of Voldemort's Horcruxes, Marvolo Gaunt's ring, destroying a piece of Voldemort's soul. Although Dumbledore's arm became all but useless, he lived on to continue leading the fight thanks to Snape's quick work.

At his home in Spinner's End the summer before Harry's sixth year, Snape was visited by Narcissa Malfoy and Bellatrix Lestrange, mother and aunt respectively to Snape's student Draco Malfoy. Narcissa, believing Snape to be the best person to help her, begged Snape to help her son fulfill the task he'd been given by Voldemort, and to avoid suspicion Snape was forced to agree. Even his agreement, however, failed to convince Bellatrix (who still suspected Snape of working for Dumbledore despite Snape's flawless false explanations), and finally, backed into a corner, he was forced to make an Unbreakable Vow to Narcissa: to watch over Draco, and to complete Draco's task for him if it seemed that Draco would fail. This task, we know now, was to kill Dumbledore. Even the fight against Voldemort couldn't stop the school year from beginning or keep students away from their classes, and following the departure of

Dolores Umbridge and the reinstatement of Dumbledore, Snape was finally given the position he had sought for so long: teaching Defense Against the Dark Arts. Horace Slughorn, Snape's predecessor as both Potions Master and the head of Slytherin House, reluctantly came out of retirement to fill Snape's former position.

It was during this year that Harry came into possession of Snape's old Potions textbook, something Snape suspected when he discovered that Harry had used the dangerous spell *Sectumsempra*, which Snape himself had created as a boy, on Draco. He could not, however, confirm it, as Harry (still distrustful of him despite all evidence to the contrary) was able to hide it.

With the Unbreakable Vow never far from his thoughts, Snape actively tried to convince Draco to let him help with his task in hopes of finding a way out of killing Dumbledore, but never managed to do so. By the end of the school year, Draco Malfoy had devised a way to bring Death Eaters into Hogwarts and fulfill his task on his own. Facing a weakened Dumbledore at the top of the Astronomy Tower, Draco had the older wizard at his mercy. When Snape arrived, he found a handful of Death Eaters and Draco, wand poised but unable to complete the task Voldemort had given him. Looking at Snape, Dumbledore pleaded, "'Severus . . . please . . . ,'" begging Snape to do what the old wizard knew that Snape had to, as much as he hated the very idea: end Dumbledore's life. And then, to maintain his cover, to ensure that the Order would have a source on the inside for the bigger battles still to come, Snape did his duty, using the unforgivable *Avada Kedavra* so that there would be no mistake, as much as the "revulsion and hatred etched in the harsh lines of his face" revealed that he did not want to commit this crime (*Half-Blood Prince* 595).

Although the fact that Dumbledore died due to Snape's actions cannot be disputed, this heinous act was done for the greater good, not only with Dumbledore's consent but at his insistence. Tragically, that knowledge belonged to Snape and Dumbledore alone. Snape's sacrifice included more than Dumbledore's life; Snape gave up his respected place on the Hogwarts faculty, his long-sought Defense Against the Dark Arts position, and his status among his peers.

Snape fled as soon as Dumbledore disappeared off the edge of the tower, accompanying Draco out of the castle to a place where they would be able to Disapparate. Harry, having just seen Snape kill

Dumbledore and unaware of Snape and Dumbledore's agreement, furiously pursued him, but the professor blocked every curse Harry cast and even told him what he was doing wrong—giving Harry one final lesson to help him in his continuing fight against Lord Voldemort. Insisting to the Death Eaters who wanted to kill Harry that the boy "belongs to the Dark Lord" and thus protecting Harry as well as he was able, he departed Hogwarts with those who believed him to be a hero to their cause, surrounded by the enemies that he had worked against for so long.

---

## FOUND: Black iPod. Men's underwear department, Dark Marks & Spencer, Hogsmeade. Music listed below. Floo Joyce Millman to claim.

"I Put a Spell on You"

"That Old Black Magic"

"Strange Brew"

"Prince of Darkness"

"If You're Feeling Sinister"

"Paint It, Black"

"Union of the Snake"

"If You Could Read My Mind"

"The Memory Remains"

"Pictures of Lily"

"James"

"Can't Get It Out of My Head"

"Cold Cold Heart"

"Cruel to Be Kind"

"Spies"

"Under Pressure"

"The Great Pretender"

"Spiderwebs"

"Paranoid"

"Lonely"

"Mr. Lonely"

"So Lonely"

"Only the Lonely"

"Alone Again, Naturally"

"Wanted Dead or Alive"

"Hate Me"

"Pain"

"Hurt"

"Creep"

"Loser"

*The Best of the Smiths, Volume I*

---

# IV.
# ALAN RICKMAN:
# THE PERFECT CHOICE
# FOR A RELUCTANT
# HERO

All the world's a stage
And all the men and women merely players;
They have their exits and their entrances,
And one man in his time plays many parts . . .

—JAQUES, *As You Like It*, Act II, Scene vii

AS WE WONDER ABOUT what role Severus Snape will play on the Harry Potter stage in the final installment, we can examine the choice made for the actor to portray him in the film series for clues just as we look inside the books themselves.

Alan Rickman, our on-screen Snape, has a long résumé of reluctant hero characters, characters whose situations and motivations resonate with Snape's. Shakespeare's *Troilus and Cressida*[1] might seem to be about, well, *Troilus and Cressida*, but much of the story centers on the persuasion of Achilles by Nestor and Ulysses to join his fellow Greeks in battle against the Trojans, and Rickman played the proud yet reluctant warrior Achilles in a 1985 Royal Shakespeare Company stage production. Snape, prouder than even Achilles, also needed some persuasion, from Dumbledore, to carry out certain tasks, a reservation we learn about in *Half-Blood Prince*. Will Snape, like Achilles, end his story as much a hero as Achilles did?

As you may have guessed from the quote above, Rickman also played the melancholy Jaques in the comedy *As You Like It* for the Royal Shakespeare Company, dressing the fool and reveling in misery while his fellows celebrate. Rickman's Snape dresses as the villain, but his actions speak otherwise, and his role as a player on this stage is still shrouded in mystery. Which leads us to what it is about Rickman that makes him the ideal Snape: he is a master at understatement, of hinting at deep feeling behind a sardonic mask. Because, as Rickman knows from the Potter creator herself, there is far more to Snape than meets the eye.

### The Romantic Leading Man?

Absolutely! While it may be nearly impossible to imagine Snape as a romantic character (legions of fan fiction writers, photograph manipulators, and fan artists excepted, of course), Alan Rickman is well known

---

[1] *Troilus and Cressida* also features Helen of Troy among its characters, whose daughter's name was, coincidentally, Hermione.

for his roles in love stories on stage and screen, from Romeo in *Romeo and Juliet* and Ferdinand in *The Tempest* early in his career to the more recent (and Tony-nominated) portrayal of Elyot Chase in *Private Lives*. According to one female fan quoted in a September 1991 *GQ* article on Rickman, "when he played Valmont (in the play *Les Liaisons Dangereuses*) something about his passion and intelligence made him unbelievably sexy."

Rickman played Jamie in 1991's *Truly, Madly, Deeply*, called "the thinking person's *Ghost*" by the Knight-Ridder News Service in June 1991. The sardonic but loving Jamie cared so deeply for his girlfriend Nina that he returned from the grave to be with his love in this Anthony Minghella-directed film. That's some serious determination, a quality Snape would respect—and, if our theorizing proves correct and it was his love for and remose over the death of Lily Potter that drove Snape to Dumbledore's employ, the kind of love that Snape would understand.

Ang Lee's 1995 version of *Sense and Sensibility*, the Jane Austen tale of two very different sisters—practical Elinor and romantic Marianne Dashwood—and their quest for the ideal marriage, features Rickman as a truly good (if undemonstrative) man, Colonel Christopher Brandon. An old family friend, he takes an immediate liking to Marianne, possibly because she reminds him so much of the love of his youth, a young girl who he had wanted to marry but of whom his family had disapproved because she was poor. Although Marianne's heart leads her elsewhere for a time, Colonel Brandon finally wins her over, and after the wedding, she realizes that she does truly love him.

Rickman returned to the stage in 1998 to portray Marc Antony in Shakespeare's tragic love story, *Antony and Cleopatra*. A great soldier and one of the three rulers of Rome, Rickman's Antony falls in love with the beautiful Queen of Egypt. Their love leads to war, and the two star-crossed lovers both die at their own hands.

*Love, Actually* (2003) features Rickman as (ironically) Harry, the manager of a design agency who is in the midst of a mid-life crisis. His secretary, Mia, is attracted to him, and he cautiously welcomes her attentions, purchasing an expensive necklace for her for Christmas. His wife, Karen, discovers the necklace in Harry's coat pocket and assumes that it is a gift for her, but when the gifts are given Karen receives a CD instead. Although thoughtless to the effect his wandering attention is having on his wife, Harry does resist the temptation Mia presents, resisting the urge to sleep with her when the opportunity arises. The movie ends with Karen and their kids picking up Harry at an airport terminal, giving the family a chance at a happy ending; although the two have issues to work through, they intend to give their marriage a chance. Tempted by a real-life kind of "Dark," this Harry resists it.

With roles such as these on his résumé, we see the vast amount of feeling and heart that Rickman can portray. In the novels, we do not see Snape as capable of such things—at least until *Order of the Phoenix* and *Half-Blood Prince*, where we learn more about his childhood and adolescence, explaining his adult coldness, and see him demonstrating compassion toward Narcissa Malfoy. In the movies, however, Rickman's history of occasionally awkward and often conflicted leading men helps him convey that depth in Snape from the beginning—and lets us conceive of possibilities for Snape, such as loving Lily, that we otherwise might not have believed.

## The Reluctant Hero

Rickman has portrayed a host of "good guys," but with his style and manner, most don't begin that way. His characters are often self-important and sardonic, but the heart inside each of them eventually shows through.

In the comedy *Galaxy Quest* (1999), Rickman plays actor Alexander Dane, a cynical Shakespearean actor who became typecast by playing the half-human Dr. Lazarus on a *Star Trek*-like television show. Despising his fame but continuing to appear in Dr. Lazarus's make-up for fans because it pays the bills, he grudgingly repeats overwritten lines such as, "By Grabthar's hammer, by the sons of Worvan, you shall be avenged!" It's no wonder Dane was a bit grumpy.

The focus of the fictional show, and of its fans, is Tim Allen's egocentric Jason Nesmith, a.k.a. Commander Peter Quincy Taggart, the star and hero. Nesmith's fame and attitude contributed a great deal to Dane's frustration, anger, and resentment. Sound familiar? Think of Snape's resentment of popular James Potter, the star at Hogwarts during Snape's time as a student despite his many misdeeds. Snape, although more talented, was unpopular, abnormal, and ignored—when he wasn't being bullied. Snape's hatred of Harry, due to Snape's assumption that Harry is like James in his egocentric attitude—"'You might be laboring under the delusion that the entire wizarding world is impressed with you,' Snape went on, so quietly that no one else could hear him . . . 'but I don't care how many times your picture appears in the papers'" (*Goblet of Fire* 516)—is echoed in Dane's accusation of Nesmith: "Oh, of course! IT'S ALL ABOUT YOU, ISN'T IT?"

Dane eventually finds someone who believes in him, the (actual) alien Quillek, and suddenly he becomes capable of great things, including the toughest act of all: forgiveness (something Snape hasn't yet been able to master, but may be destined for in Book Seven). He mends the bridge between himself and Nesmith, which leads to one additional Snape parallel: Dane pretending to battle Nesmith in order to convince a group of villainous aliens that they are enemies when they are actually setting a trap. If we are correct about Snape's motivations, when *Half-Blood Prince* comes to the big screen, this false enmity will be in full force when Snape and Dumbledore face each other at the top of the tower.

Rickman played the Metatron in 1999's *Dogma*, the angel who, as he explains, "acts as the voice of God. Any documented occasion when some yahoo claims God has spoken to them, they're speaking to me. Or they're talking to themselves." Serving primarily as Exposition Guy, he is sardonic yet sensible (with an occasional craving for Mexican food), and though he can be abrasive—he is definitely on the side of good—he successfully nudges Bethany, the last scion of Jesus, on to her journey so that she can save the world. The Metatron's role in Bethany's journey echoes Snape's in Harry's: Snape's job, as Harry's teacher, is to prepare Harry to face Voldemort—even if Harry doesn't find the experience of being taught particularly pleasant.

2001's *Blow Dry* featured Rickman as Phil Allen, a (surprise!) sardonic, bitter former hairdressing champion who stepped out of that life to become a small-town bartender after he felt betrayed by his wife and his hair model when they ran off together. When the annual British Hairdressing Championship descends on his town, he not only stops a competitor and former nemesis from cheating (much like Snape stopped Quirrell during the Quidditch match), but steps in for the final round to win the competition, facing long-held grudges against his teammates to do so—just as Snape will have to do with Harry if they are to defeat Voldemort for good.

Heroes don't always fit the Superman-like stereotype; they don't have to be gallant, extroverted, friendly, or even nice. A hero rises to the occasion and does what must be done no matter what the circumstances, and Rickman portrays that journey perfectly every time.

## Other Notable Roles

Rickman's roles vary widely, and not all fall under the category of Romantic Leading Man, Reluctant Hero, or of course, Villain. In these roles, we still can find reflections of the Snape he has created on-screen.

For example, in 2004, Rickman starred alongside Mos Def in the HBO drama *Something the Lord Made*. As Dr. Alfred Blalock, a respected doctor in the American south in the 1940s, he works with African-American lab technician Vivien Thomas on a new technique for helping babies with heart problems. Despite impressive, innovative results that should have been applauded throughout the medical world, they are forced to fight the prejudices against them. Similarly, Snape also must work despite the prejudices against him due to his former affiliation, enduring the distrust of his peers.

Snape's resentment is portrayed perfectly through Rickman's voice and inflections, especially when completing tasks he feels are beneath him. He uses this tone to the extreme as the voice of Marvin the Paranoid Android in 2005's *The Hitchhiker's Guide to the Galaxy*: "I've been ordered to take you down to the bridge. Here I am, brain the size of a planet, and they ask me to take you down to the bridge. Call that job satisfaction? 'Cause I don't."

Alan Rickman's brilliance as an actor makes Snape come alive, sometimes in unexpected ways. There is, after all, so much about Snape we do not yet know—but Rickman does. As Rickman himself revealed to *Handbag* in November 2003, "There are such still waters in there. And the trouble is that there's so much we don't know yet 'cause J. K. Rowling hasn't revealed it. I know a couple of things about all that, that you don't and I'm not telling. . . ."

# V.
# SLYTHERIN HOUSE: NOT (ALWAYS) EVIL

You are seeing Slytherin [H]ouse always from the perspective of Death Eaters' children. They are a small fraction of the total Slytherin population. I'm not saying all the other Slytherins are adorable, but they're certainly not Draco, they're certainly not, you know, Crabbe and Goyle. They're not all like that; that would be too brutal for words, wouldn't it?

—J. K. ROWLING, online interview with
The Leaky Cauldron and MuggleNet, July 2005

THE SCHOOL SYSTEM AT HOGWARTS might seem as foreign to some readers as the rest of the wizarding world, but the basis for Hogwarts is fully grounded in the Muggle world: the English public boarding school. The English system of Houses and prefects continues to this day in many boarding schools all across the world, and many of these schools have long histories to rival Hogwarts itself, such as Eton College, founded in 1440 by King Henry VI; Winchester College, founded in the fourteenth century by William of Wykeham, Bishop of Winchester and Chancellor to Richard II; and Harrow School, founded in 1572 under the Royal Charter granted by Elizabeth I to farmer John Lyon.

Many of these boarding schools rely on some sort of House system. Some schools have the House name as only a team label, the title of a living space, or for other administrative purposes, while other schools divide up students into Houses based on age alone. However, the most common House system is the all-age sort we see at Hogwarts.

Unlike Muggle schools, the separation into Houses at Hogwarts is not set by random chance or determined administratively in any way. The Sorting Hat bases its decisions on four character traits: courage for Gryffindor, loyalty for Hufflepuff, intelligence for Ravenclaw, and ambition for Slytherin.

While it's tempting to call all Gryffindors "good" and all Slytherins "bad," it is in how these traits are applied that make a person "good" or "bad," not the qualities themselves. It would be all too easy to rate all Gryffindors as "good," all Slytherins as "bad," and all Ravenclaws and Hufflepuffs as generally neutral. Rowling installed this House-based categorization method immediately so that readers would know who they should root for and who they should despise. And, indeed, for many of the events and situations in Rowling's books, these categorizations remain fairly accurate. But such easy categorizations aren't *always* accurate.

This becomes particularly true as Harry ages, the divisions between the Houses becoming more and more indistinct, and as we learn more about the Harry Potter universe, the lines between black and white blur at an ever-increasing rate. While House membership is an easy way to categorize the characters, all four Houses have inherent worth; the school values all four traits. Loyalty to House and school, courage in daily life and on the Quidditch field, excellence in studies, and a drive to succeed are qualities that every student at Hogwarts should possess. Many wizards and witches who once called Slytherin home have become perfectly "good," esteemed members of society; remember, Slytherin members count for one out of every four wizards and witches educated at Hogwarts, and one out of every four Hogwarts graduates certainly didn't become a Death Eater.

Slytherin, of course, is the House with the worst reputation: it's the House into which Voldemort was sorted, and the House most of the Death Eaters were in during their time at Hogwarts. And to make that reputation seem even worse, Slytherin House prefers pure-blooded wizards, an attitude that makes readers distrust members of Slytherin even more. However, when Hogwarts would have been founded a thousand years ago, right in the middle of Europe's Dark Ages, the inclusive attitudes of Godric Gryffindor and Helga Hufflepuff would have been the exception, not the norm. We Muggles are no better; discrimination is one of our least admirable traits, and we separate based on race, class, religion, and any other way someone might seem "different." In the world of Harry Potter, all wizards and witches are considered suspect by some Muggles; as Rowling said on Salon.com in March 1999, "The wizards represent all that the true '[M]uggle' most fears: they are plainly outcasts and comfortable with being so. Nothing is more unnerving to the truly conventional than the unashamed misfit!"

Professor McGonagall, in her welcome to the first years in *Sorcerer's Stone*, claims that each House has its own noble history and that each has produced outstanding witches and wizards. Students are sorted into Houses for a reason; according to Rowling's July 2005 interview with The Leaky Cauldron and MuggleNet, not only is the Sorting Hat never wrong, but its words come from the founders themselves. The beginning of these histories was the founding of the school by four friends, each tremendous wizards or witches in their own rights. They founded the school's sorting system, and the foursome had good reason for dividing up their students as they did, be it something as simple as wanting to cultivate the quality they deemed most important.

If Slytherin were nothing more than a breeding ground for evil, the source of all Death Eaters, would Dumbledore have allowed it to continue? Of course not. If disbanding Slytherin would help in the fight against Voldemort, the House would have been disbanded years ago. Therefore Slytherin must serve a purpose and have a positive meaning in the wizarding world.

Rowling explained in that same July 2005 interview why Slytherin is so important to Hogwarts, and part of that reason is elemental: "It is the tradition to have four [H]ouses, but in this case, I wanted them to correspond roughly to the four elements. So Gryffindor is fire, Ravenclaw is air, Hufflepuff is earth, and Slytherin is water, hence the fact that their common room is under the lake. So again, it was this idea of harmony and balance, that you had four necessary components and by integrating them you would make a very strong place. But they remain fragmented, as we know." This need for balance, Rowling implies, extends beyond the four basic elements and into human nature itself.

## The Positive Side of Ambition

Ambition is the key attribute of Slytherin, first described by the Sorting Hat as the House for shrewd people who use any means necessary to achieve their ends. In a word, they are ambitious. Ambition is often seen as an untrustworthy trait, and it is the only one of the four House traits that has an immediate stigma.

But while it is often discussed in a negative light, ambition itself is *not* an evil trait. Ambition is only the strong desire to achieve something, which isn't inherently bad. Ambitious people are goal-oriented, understanding what it means to focus single-mindedly on succeeding. If they want to achieve something, they do what it takes to make it happen. They reach out and grab opportunities when they appear, following the example of their serpent mascot. And when opportunities don't appear on their own, ambitious people create them.

Striving to succeed can be a good thing. Where would society be without those of great vision, striving to achieve their goals? Ambition can lead a person to creating a good life for himself and a better life for others, be they family or strangers. Ambitious people can also be very helpful people; after all, helping others can sometimes help people help themselves. Ambition can make the world a better place; it all depends on how you use it.

The biggest advantage that those in Slytherin have going for them is that they are realists. They do not wrap themselves in idealistic aspirations but rather see the world as it is and how best to use their circumstances to their advantage. They understand the value of achievement and of working to realize their goals. The challenge for those in Slytherin is to not allow their worse natures to get the best of them as they work toward their goals. What those goals are, and the path they choose to take in accomplishing those goals, is a personal choice of each student, not dictated by their House but rather by their heads and their hearts.

Those who are ambitious must be bold in pursuing their goals; with such similarities, it's easy to imagine Godric Gryffindor and Salazar Slytherin as friends. Bold Godric may have been more idealistic than his friend Salazar, but both would have possessed a similar drive to see the school they had founded succeed.

But if those sorted into Slytherin are not automatically evil, why are so many Slytherins on the side of Lord Voldemort? The sad truth is that many in Slytherin chose the easy path to power when it was offered: becoming a Death Eater, and using Voldemort's power to increase their own. It is an unfortunate side of human nature that many look for the best results from the least amount of effort, and that is what Voldemort offered. Also, although it is true that most Death Eaters called Slytherin home, that isn't the case for all of them: Peter Pettigrew, remember, belonged to Gryffindor, and Rowling stated in her 2005 interview with The Leaky Cauldron and MuggleNet after the publication of *Half-Blood Prince* that, "You will have people connected with Death Eaters in the other [H]ouses, yeah, absolutely." Slytherin is not to blame for all the evils in the world.

### The Other Side of the Serpent; Positive Symbolism throughout the World

> We must combine the toughness of the serpent with the softness of
> the dove, a tough mind and a tender heart.
> —MARTIN LUTHER KING

Many aspects of Slytherin have been set up to cause instant distrust among readers. The Slytherin House common room is located in a dungeon under the lake, and its mascot, a serpent, is almost universally reviled in our culture, as opposed to the admired lion of Harry's House, Gryffindor. But let's take a good look at this mascot and its mythological background. While serpents are associated with evil in Judaism and Christianity, snakes are more commonly seen as either beneficial or neutral in other mythologies worldwide.

The Egyptians equated serpents with the god Nehebkau, who guarded the entrance to the underworld, and they adorned the crown of the pharaoh with the figure of a cobra. In India, *nāgas*, or giant snakes, are still considered by some to be nature spirits and the protectors of springs, wells, and rivers. The Ancient Greeks and Minoans believed the serpent to be the symbol of wisdom, and indeed, even the Bible says, "Now the serpent was more cunning than any beast of the field which the Lord God has made" (Genesis 3:1). The caduceus, the image of two snakes wrapped around a winged staff, symbolizes medicine to this day.

In the Chinese Zodiac, according to the Chinese Cultural Center of San Francisco's Web site, "People born in the Year of the Snake are deep. They say little and possess great wisdom. They never have to worry about money; they are financially fortunate. Snake people are often quite vain, selfish, and a bit stingy. Yet they have tremendous sympathy for others and try to help those less fortunate. Snake people tend to overdo, since they have doubts about other people's judgment and prefer to rely on themselves. They are determined in whatever they do and hate to fail. Although calm on the surface, they are intense and passionate."

Since a snake sheds its skin and appears to renew itself, it is a symbol of regeneration and immortality in mythology throughout Europe, Africa, and even the New World. In the *Epic of Gilgamesh*, Gilgamesh dove to the bottom of the sea to find the Plant of Life. However, when he rested from his labor, a snake ate the plant before he had the chance, giving the snake "eternal life" and dooming Gilgamesh to mortality. In the form of the "Ouroboros," a snake or dragon in a perfect circle swallowing its own tail, the snake is part of one of the oldest mystical symbols in the world, appearing in mythologies throughout the world, including Aztec, Greek, Chinese, West African, and Native American.

The snake has done well for itself, deserving the honor of becoming the mascot of a House at Hogwarts. Snakes fit the description of the House as "ambitious" as well; if you've ever seen one swallow prey wider than its body, you know what I'm talking about. Talk about ambitious meals! Recently reported python meals have included an alligator, a pit bull, and a kangaroo. "Biting off more than you can chew" doesn't apply when you can swallow what you want whole.

## The Good Slytherins

While it's true that Slytherin members aren't usually the nicest folks, from the collection of Death Eaters to those who are simply spiteful or nasty (like Marcus Flint, Millicent Bulstrode, or Pansy Parkinson), we can't say the same of Slytherin members as a whole. *Half-Blood Prince* introduces us to a key Slytherin figure, new Potions Master Horace Slughorn, who is one of the few members of Slytherin who has not been portrayed in a chiefly negative light. Instead, he is depicted as neutral, if not slightly positive.

While Slughorn becomes questionable to the reader, just as he does to Harry, the moment that we learn of his House affiliation, his ambitious nature lends itself more to "networking" than anything else upon his return to Hogwarts. He seeks out students—from all four Houses—who appear to have the potential for greatness and invites them into the Slug Club, his own unofficial honor society in which they get a chance to know each other, successful past Slug Club members, and, perhaps most importantly, him. Slughorn judges on merit, not by family or House, and he favors those with talent and ability. Thus Slughorn creates a positive networking environment, wizard-style. While he benefits in small ways from starting so many careers, the members of the Slug Club seem to be the true winners. Just like in our Muggle society, who you know is often far more important that what you know.

Unlike many better-known Slytherins, Slughorn has no trouble accepting and befriending successful Muggle-born witches and wizards such as Hermione, nor does he appear to show any animosity toward those outside of the Slytherin House. Slughorn may sometimes be selfish, superficial, snobbish, materialistic, and deceptive, but he is also pleasant, without prejudice to those of "impure" blood, and loyal to Dumbledore. He may be occasionally irritating, given to name dropping and long speeches about his past students, but he's a good teacher, and disapproves of fellow Slytherins who associate with Voldemort, going so far as to exclude the children of Death Eaters from his Slug Club regardless of how talented or well-connected they may be. He feels guilty about his role in aiding Voldemort in his rise to power, however small, and when pressed by Harry eventually gives up the unaltered memory of his conversation with the young Voldemort despite the potential cost to his reputation.

Theodore Nott is one of the few other Slytherins who we've met who may show another side of the House. He is not friends with Malfoy and other Slytherin students. In *Order of the Phoenix*, Theodore is seen in the library with Crabbe, Goyle, and Draco looking very angry at Harry as he walks by, but Harry has just (rightly) named all four of their fathers as Death Eaters in *The Quibbler*. That is, however, the worst light in which Theodore is ever shown, and it seems that much of his story has gone untold. According to Rowling in her 2005 Leaky Cauldron/MuggleNet interview, "I know much more about Theodore Nott than has ever appeared in the books. Raised by a very elderly widower and Death Eater father, Theodore is a clever loner who does not feel the need to join gangs, including Malfoy's."

Phineas Nigellus Black, more commonly referred to as Phineas Nigellus, is another unusual Slytherin. The great-great-grandfather of Sirius Black, he is reputed to be the least popular headmaster Hogwarts ever had—until Dolores Umbridge came along, that is. His portrait hangs both in Dumbledore's office and at 12 Grimmauld Place, and while he was a terrible headmaster and serves the current headmaster only reluctantly, he still provides a conduit between Hogwarts and the headquarters of the Order of the Phoenix. He also calls Harry out when he acts rashly, bringing him back to earth and stopping him from fleeing in *Order of the Phoenix*:

> "I thought," said Phineas Nigellus, stroking his pointed beard, "that to belong in Gryffindor House you were supposed to be *brave*? It looks to me as though you would have been better off in my own house. We Slytherins are brave, yes, but not stupid. For instance, given the choice, we will always choose to save our own necks."

"It's not my own neck I'm saving," said Harry tersely, tugging the trunk over a patch of particularly uneven, moth-eaten carpet right in front of the door.

"Oh, I see," said Phineas Nigellus, still stroking his beard. "This is no cowardly flight—you are being *noble*" (494-495).

Also, unlike the other members of his family, one of which committed the murder, Phineas Nigellus was saddened to learn of Sirius's death.

While certainly a villain through and through, Draco Malfoy creates another interesting case. While we despise him for how he treats Harry as well as for being generally despicable, he steps up in a way that is almost admirable when he tries to take his father's place in the Death Eaters after Lucius is imprisoned. Of course, his assigned task of killing Dumbledore makes us hate him all the more. But, as malicious as he generally is, his assigned task was too horrible for even him to bear; in the end, he fails to follow through in killing Dumbledore, despite having the older wizard at his mercy.

Of course, Draco's hatred of Harry, something he shares with many of the other members of Slytherin, is perhaps the biggest reason for us to dislike this House, but their hatred is not irritational. It's not even an indication of the House aligning with Voldemort. Remember, Draco treated Harry well at their first meeting, before Harry chose to align with those Draco considered inferior. Also, had Harry been sorted into Slytherin (as was almost the case: "'Not Slytherin, eh? . . . Are you sure? You could be great, you know, it's all here in your head, and Slytherin will help you on the way to greatness, no doubt about that—no? Well, if you're sure . . .'" the Sorting Hat told Harry on page 121 of *Sorcerer's Stone*), he would have been a very popular person there. Harry is, after all, "the Boy Who Lived" and "the Chosen One," and titles such as those come with instant fame and an automatic reputation of power, both of which would appeal to Slytherins. Not having that status, or at the very least, access to it, can cause resentment, and when children are resentful, they get mean.

And if we are correct in our theorizing of his innocence, Severus Snape, the now-former head of Slytherin, has shown perhaps the greatest courage and strength of spirit of all. Despite his dislike for Harry, Snape has protected him surreptitiously when necessary for years, from saving him from Quirrell's jinx in *Sorcerer's Stone* to sending the order to the Ministry of Magic after him in *Order of the Phoenix*. He has earned

# Speculations

## Has Snape Ever Loved Anyone?

Hogwarts is an oddly monastic environment. The only incidence of hanky-panky among the adults is Hagrid's courtship of Madame Maxime, the headmistress of Beauxbatons. If any of the teachers are married, we have yet to meet or even hear about their spouses. J. K. Rowling was asked about this in a Q&A session with fans in 2001. She answered that "a few" Hogwarts staffers are married "but that information is sort of restricted—you'll find out." Earlier, in a 1999 interview, when asked if Snape was going to fall in love, she replied that the thought of Snape in love was a "very horrible idea" and promised that we would find out why in Book Seven. Is it such a horrible idea because he's incapable of falling in love—or because he's already married?

Alas, there are no clues in the books so far to suggest that Snape has a secret wife stashed in his dungeon. Nor is there any evidence supporting the fan theory that the Potions Master was married when he was a Death Eater and that the death of his wife had something to do with him turning against Voldemort.

Could Snape have once been in love with Lily Potter? Maybe. A full-blown reciprocal love seems unlikely; Lily was James Potter's girl. But Snape might well have had a teenage crush on her. Rowling tells us in the books that many boys were smitten with Lily; she was vivacious and popular. She was also uncommonly kind, as Lupin tells Harry in the film adaptation of *Harry Potter and the Prisoner of Azkaban*. Perhaps Lily extended that kindness to the weird outcast Snape. Lily and Snape were both skilled at potion-making; this mutual interest could have resulted in a (probably clandestine) friendship that stopped far short of love (at least on Lily's part). As we discuss in this book's essay "In Defense of Snape," he insults James throughout the saga, but never insults Lily. More strangely, he never even mentions her name. Has he removed these troublesome memories? Possibly—Snape is disdainful of "'fools who wear their hearts proudly on their sleeves,'" as he tells Harry during their Occlumency lessons (*Order of the Phoenix* 536). Maybe Lily recalls vulnerable emotions on which a person in Snape's delicate position as a double agent can't afford to dwell.

## Has Snape Ever Loved Anyone? (Con't.)

While it's hard to imagine the icy, sardonic Snape wooing anybody, he does reveal a glimmer of tenderness in the "Spinner's End" chapter of *Half-Blood Prince*, when he agrees to Narcissa Malfoy's tearful plea for help. Is Snape just a big dumb softie underneath it all, melting at the tears of a beautiful blonde? The intriguing interplay between Snape and Narcissa in this chapter raises the possibility that Snape does indeed have a romantic streak, and that he is not immune to female charms.

Love is a two-way street. We suspect that Snape loved someone in his life, but has someone ever loved him? In a 2005 interview with staffers from two popular Harry Potter Web sites, Rowling affirmed that Snape has been loved. But she would not elaborate. The only thing we can say for certain is that the sallow, hook-nosed greasy git has a face that only a mother could love.

Dumbledore's complete trust, including a position at Hogwarts, even after his tenure as a Death Eater. Most impressive of all, he has served as a double agent on behalf of the *Order of the Phoenix*, and while his true allegiance has never been made public, Snape has perhaps done more to fight Lord Voldemort than anyone. Although Dumbledore died at his hands, that death may have served a greater purpose and been almost as great of a sacrifice for Snape as it was for Dumbledore.

Without Slytherin, we would be far more than simply short a few villains and questionable characters. Hogwarts would be less interesting, and, more importantly, far less real. Wizards are human, just like us Muggles, and we're not all strong-hearted, loyal, or brilliant. Sometimes, our strengths lie elsewhere, whether in capitalizing on opportunities or creating them for ourselves. We need Slytherin in order to recognize that part of ourselves, the part that can be selfish or self-serving but, if we're careful, be used for positive ends rather than evil ones. After all, as Rowling said in the 2005 Leaky Cauldron/MuggleNet interview, "You have to embrace all of a person, you have to take them with their flaws, and everyone's got them. It's the same way with the student body. If only they could achieve perfect unity, you would have an absolute unstoppable force, and I suppose it's that craving for unity and wholeness that means that they keep that quarter of the school that maybe does not encapsulate the most generous and noble qualities, in the hope, in the very Dumbledore-esque hope that they will achieve union, and they will achieve harmony. Harmony is the word."

# VI.
# WHO IS SNAPE?

*Orson Scott Card*

MOST OF THE HARRY POTTER NOVELS are self-contained. You can read them without having read any previous volumes in the series, since the author provides you with reminders of all significant events that have gone before. And when each volume ends, the major issues raised in that book have been resolved.

Always there is the continuing expectation of a final confrontation between Harry Potter and Lord Voldemort, of course, with other questions and puzzles along the way. But the reader feels, at the end of each book, that *this* story, at least, has ended.

Not so with the sixth volume, *Harry Potter and the Half-Blood Prince*. A series that had been steadily darkening in tone—growing up, in a way, along with its hero—with this volume darkened in another way: it seemed to some that we actually knew less about what was going on at the end of that book than we did at the beginning.

We are left dangling, with Harry in more peril than ever, Voldemort stronger than ever, the quest that has driven the story leading apparently to nothing, and Dumbledore dead.[1]

But the biggest puzzle at the end of *Half-Blood Prince* is Professor Severus Snape. The head of Slytherin House at Hogwarts, Snape bears the sinister mark of Voldemort on his forearm and was one of the Death Eaters during Voldemort's previous bid for supremacy in the magical world.

We have learned that he functions as a double agent, pretending to be Voldemort's loyal servant, spying on Dumbledore, Hogwarts, and the Order of the Phoenix, while in fact he is really Dumbledore's agent, spying on Voldemort and the Death Eaters. Or is it the other way around? Is he only pretending to Dumbledore that he is only pretending to be loyal to Voldemort? The questions become, as they always do with double agents, quite circular and unanswerable, until you see what the double agent does in a crisis.

---

[1] Though we must remember that dead things do live on in the world of Harry Potter. Rowling has been quoted as saying that Dumbledore is most definitely dead, and the fact that his face appears in a portrait in the headmaster's office at Hogwarts seems proof enough that his death is genuine. Also, as Dumbledore himself has said, "'No spell can reawaken the dead'" (*Goblet of Fire* 697).

But what if "really dead" doesn't necessarily mean "gone"? Isn't Fawkes the phoenix really dead before he rises from the ashes of his immolation? While it is unlikely that Dumbledore would fear death enough to choose to remain a ghost, it is possible that there is some deep magic involving the phoenix that rises from the flames of Dumbledore's funeral pyre just before the table on which the body lay is enclosed

Well, we have that answer, don't we? In the climactic scene, Snape kills Dumbledore, which seems to most to be conclusive proof of his perfidy. And yet . . . we also have reason to believe that what Snape does, Dumbledore wanted him to do—that by killing Dumbledore, he is actually furthering Dumbledore's plan.

It was important to Dumbledore that it *not* be Draco Malfoy who slew him—that Draco be protected from Voldemort, along with his whole malicious family. And Dumbledore is so determined to die (or is it just to keep Harry Potter safe?) that he puts Harry under a spell of immobility—and under his Invisibility Cloak—during the crisis atop the tower. Dumbledore wanted *no one* to be in a position to prevent his death.

Yet what do we make of the critical moment?

> "Severus . . ."
> The sound frightened Harry beyond anything he had experienced all evening. For the first time, Dumbledore was pleading (*Half-Blood Prince* 595).

Pleading? One assumes—Harry assumes—that he is pleading for Snape to save him, or at least to refrain from killing him.

But he might just as easily be pleading for him to do a thing that he knows Snape does not want to do: kill him before Draco can, so that Voldemort's plan to make a murderer of the boy will fail.

Snape approaches Dumbledore, pushing Draco "roughly" out of the way. Is that roughness to show his scorn for Draco's inability to commit murder? Or is it a bit of theatre, to make the others think that he scorns Draco when in fact he is making sure Draco is not in a position to change his mind and kill?

---

in a stone tomb. Could there be a good-magic equivalent of the dark-magic Horcrux—a survival of the soul on earth in a form that can return? Could it be that when Dumbledore says that as long as anyone at Hogwarts is loyal to him, he will not really be gone, he means it literally?

The evidence for the possibility of Dumbledore rising like a phoenix is not direct—how could it be, without Rowling tipping her hand?—but it is enough that if Dumbledore *does* show up again, alive, the readers will nod and say, "Yes, of course." In short, there is no particular reason to think that Dumbledore alone should be irrevocably, invisibly, and silently dead.

Snape gazed for a moment at Dumbledore, and there was revulsion and hatred etched in the harsh lines of his face.

"Severus . . . please . . ."

Snape raised his wand and pointed it directly at Dumbledore.

"*Avada Kedavra!*" (*Half-Blood Prince* 595–596).

What does that look of revulsion and hatred mean?

Is it long pent-up resentment of and malice toward Dumbledore, which Snape is finally free to show as he murders the man he has pretended to serve?

Is it Harry's imperfect ability to interpret the meaning of Snape's facial expression? Harry has long since lost the ability to assign any positive meaning to any act, statement, or expression of Snape's. Is Harry simply wrong?

Is Snape's expression of hatred and revulsion merely theatre, a display for the benefit of the other Death Eaters beside him on the tower?

Or are his hatred and revulsion sincere enough, but caused by the violent act he is about to perform, the loathsome spell he is about to cast, the disloyalty that his loyalty is causing him to display?

Is it that revulsion—at the idea of killing Dumbledore using a forbidden curse—that causes Dumbledore to plead with him? Perhaps Dumbledore's "'Severus . . . please . . .'" is saying, in effect, I know you hate to do this, my friend, but please, overcome your revulsion and kill me in a way that will save Draco and win you Voldemort's utter trust.

Likewise, when Snape—still sneering—blocks Harry's attempts to use the unforgivable Cruciatus Curse, not just against himself but against another Death Eater, is he thwarting Harry as an enemy, or keeping the boy from turning himself into something evil by using such a terrible curse—the way he shields Draco in the tower?

After all, as Harry casts spell after spell at him, Snape does not fight back—though Harry urges him to. Instead he blocks all of Harry's spells before he can cast them.

"'Blocked again and again and again until you learn to keep your mouth shut and your mind closed, Potter!'" (*Half-Blood Prince* 603). Who is speaking here? The Snape who taunts Harry Potter—the Snape who has just said, "'Coward, did you call me, Potter? . . . Your father would never attack me unless it was four on one, what would you call him, I wonder?'" (*Half-Blood Prince* 603). Or the Snape who is a very demanding teacher, warning Harry which skills he will have to master before he can hope to be effective against Voldemort?

When the Cruciatus Curse is cast against Harry, he assumes it is Snape who did it—but no, it is Snape who ends it and insists that the other Death Eaters respect Voldemort's order that "'Potter belongs to the Dark Lord—we are to leave him!'" (*Half-Blood Prince* 603). But is he just obeying Voldemort? Or saving Harry Potter according to Dumbledore's plan?

In the aftermath, when Harry tells the remaining faculty what Snape did to Dumbledore, they all believe that Snape is therefore a murderer and a sincere Death Eater. But Rowling is careful to remind us, in McGonagall's words, "'Snape. . . . We all wondered . . . but he [Dumbledore] trusted . . . always . . . *Snape* . . . I can't believe it . . .'" (*Half-Blood Prince* 615).

Are we to believe what they all believe, that Snape is guilty? Or are we to heed McGonagall's unwitting advice, "I can't believe it"?

As if to make sure we got the point, Rowling has Tonks say, "'But Dumbledore swore he was on our side! . . . I always thought Dumbledore must know something about Snape that we didn't . . .'" (*Half-Blood Prince* 615).

Of course, immediately after this, Harry Potter offers what he thinks was Dumbledore's "'ironclad reason'" for trusting Snape—a reason that doesn't seem so ironclad in retrospect. As Lupin points out, "'Dumbledore believed Snape was sorry James [Harry's father] was dead? Snape *hated* James . . .'" (*Half-Blood Prince* 616).

And thus Rowling tosses us back and forth. We know whom to *like*; we even know, mostly, who is honest and means what he or she says. What we don't know is who is *right*.

If one thing has been clear throughout the series, it is that Dumbledore trusts Snape; could he have been wrong? And even if Dumbledore was right to trust Snape's loyalty so far, can Snape be trusted to continue to serve Dumbledore even after Dumbledore is dead?

## The Author and the Character

In one sense, the definitive answer can only be found by reading the final volume in the series.

After all, these books have an author, and the author is free to have her characters do whatever she wants them to do. Until Rowling's words on paper turn into scenes in our minds as we read them, the answer to that question might still turn out either way—or some twisted combination of tortured moral reasoning and contradictory actions on Snape's part that keeps us guessing right to, or even past, the end.

Or is she really free to do just *anything*?

There is a logic to how a literary character is formed, especially by a writer of such visceral power as Rowling has turned out to be.

I think the power of the Harry Potter books surprised even Rowling. Certainly there is a progression of tone from the first volumes through the later ones. I spoke before of darkening, but it might rather be viewed as a de-lightening. The first volume is like J. R. R. Tolkien's *The Hobbit* in that it is self-consciously a *children's* book, full of delightful jokes. Dumbledore, like the wizard Gandalf in *The Hobbit*, is a trickster, a jester. The world is full of wonders that are, quite simply, fun; game-playing and riddle-solving are at the heart of the story. It is a romp. Even including the climax, the book is light—in physical weight, in voice, in mood, and in moral consequence.

But the later volumes have steadily progressed to ever-more-serious consequences, with ever-fewer moments of genuine frivolity. There is still humor, but it has a darker edge.

Why?

Because Rowling is no longer telling a children's story, she is telling a story that happens to be about children. The light tale-for-children tone has turned into the much darker hues of a story rising out of the author's unconscious.

Much has been said about how Rowling had the whole series planned from the beginning. I believe that this is true—up to a point. The asymmetry in the lengths of the books suggests that Rowling began to fill her pages, not with deliberate (and intellectual) inventions, but with story that simply flowed and often went in directions that simply felt right to her.

Most important, she went from the sharp, clear black-and-white morality of the first book to a far more shaded and nuanced view of good versus evil. You can almost always tell good guys from bad guys in *Sorcerer's Stone* because good guys are nice to Harry and bad guys are mean.

But by the time we find our way through *Prisoner of Azkaban*, we have a "good guy"—Sirius Black—who had been, as a student, perfectly capable of setting up the probable murder of his fellow student Severus Snape. Yet Black remains on the good-guy team.

Harry himself becomes morally ambiguous. His "pranks" and sneaking and spying may always have, in his mind, good motives, but they don't always have good consequences, and while he is not motivated by pure malice, he does delight in the occasional malicious prank.

More to the point, on many of the occasions where Snape accuses Harry of having done something dire, Harry is in fact guilty of rule-breaking or worse. Harry cooperates in crimes, like hiding and helping smuggle Hagrid's illegal dragon out of Hogwarts, and he almost never calls on even the most trusted authorities to help him. We see his deeds, correctly, as heroic—but they could also, without much twisting, be made to prove that, as Snape accuses, Harry Potter believes that he is above the law—that he is free to pick and choose which rules to obey, depending on what seems good to him at the moment, based only on the information he has.

We might be glad that Harry cheats in order to prevail in the Triwizard Tournament in *Goblet of Fire*—and it would take a moral cretin not to see that Harry's noble behavior in putting the lives of others ahead of his own chance of victory certainly earns him absolution for his rule-bending. But the fact remains: Harry Potter's larger motives might be good, but he is dangerous; he never has complete information, and yet frequently puts his own moral judgment ahead of public laws and wiser people's advice.

This is not uncommon in fiction—how many hard-boiled detectives are barely distinguishable from the criminals they pursue? The difference between a knight and a thug is often merely the color of his armor.

What makes Harry's moral ambiguity interesting is that Rowling *points it out*. Harry is the hero, but he does not always do the right thing, either in the moral or the practical sense. And characters like Snape and Draco Malfoy may be cruel and malicious, but they do not always do the *wrong* thing.

The result is that the moral universe of the Harry Potter novels has moved from clarity to a deepening *chiaroscuro* in which truth can lurk in shadows and error can stand in the sun. This is the kind of thing that authors rarely plan; it happens when they themselves become immersed in the tales and let their unconscious mind lead them down paths they had not anticipated.

So . . . what is Snape?

A character that has been planned from the beginning to act in certain ways, so that we can see the careful hand of the author preparing him for his role in the final scenes of the final book?

Or is he a character that serves a useful function in the earlier books, is almost abandoned when other characters serve that function better, but then reemerges from the author's unconscious into a powerful role that expresses her deep inner conviction that it is nearly impossible to judge ultimate moral worth solely from outward behavior?

There are two logics working here:

1. The character is the servant of the story. The author has certain jobs that need to be done in a tale, and devises characters to carry out those jobs. The characters, then, follow an *artistic* logic.

2. The author is also the servant of her own most deeply held beliefs—the things that she believes without even knowing that she believes them. Characters that endure in a well-made work of fiction are invariably captured by the author's unconscious and bent in ways that the author might not have predicted. Thus the logic that drives the character—the system of cause-and-effect demonstrated in the character's choices—is governed, not entirely by a conscious, artistic plan, but also by the author's inner imperative to create a fictional world that demonstrates the secret moral and causal universe in which she lives.

In other words, the first logic shows us the author's conscious choices—what the author believes that she believes. The second logic is where the genius rather than mere cleverness comes into play: it shows us what the author believes without knowing that it is possible to believe anything else.

Look at how the pivotal character of Gollum grows in Tolkien's classic tales of Middle-earth. In *The Hobbit*, Gollum exists for one purpose: to give Bilbo the Ring. But he is an intriguing character; for reasons Tolkien himself doesn't understand, he *matters*. In fact, he functions as an anti-hobbit, a creature much like Bilbo but the moral opposite.

# The Case for Snape's Innocence

When Tolkien set his hand to writing the sequel to *The Hobbit*, at first he only knew that he wanted to have hobbits meet Tom Bombadil, and so he put together a traveling party and sent them into the Old Forest where they met the characters about whom Tolkien had been writing poems for many years. And then . . . nothing. He had nowhere for them to go, nothing for them to do. And as many readers have felt, what he'd already had them do was nearly nothing—it was hard to care much. The events were just one thing after another.

This version of the opening of *Fellowship of the Ring* was the draft that followed artistic logic alone. And, as almost always happens, the draft was empty. Artistic logic does not create great stories, only outlines of stories.

Then, as Tolkien famously explained, he got to the inn at Bree and met a character named Strider. Strider intrigued him—an unconscious, visceral response—and in figuring out who Strider was and what he was doing, Tolkien found the *real* story of Lord of the Rings.

Still, he left that story—empty section intact, making only one significant change in the story flow. He had Gandalf tell Frodo the story of the original finding of the Ring by Deagol and Smeagol—and told of how Smeagol became Gollum.

In other words, the only change in that opening sequence that was required to make the novel satisfy that inner, unconscious logic, was to move Gollum to the center of the tale. He is not the hero; nor is he the monster. Instead, he is the center of moral ambiguity, the character who, seeming evil, might also serve the good. Other, lesser characters might also show moral ambiguity (one thinks of Saruman, Theoden, and Denethor), but none are as central to the story as Gollum.

Snape, I believe, is the Gollum of the Harry Potter books. Born at first to be little more than a convenient obstacle and a red herring, he graduates to become the center of moral ambiguity. We cannot know (as we could not with Gollum) which way he will turn. We have seen his malice, but much of it has been justified—he was more victim than victimizer in his school days, and it was "good guys" who oppressed him. So as we prepare for the final volume in the series, we can see that everything comes down to this: What choice will Snape make?

I do not anticipate that Rowling will push Snape through all of Gollum's paces: Gollum ends up choosing evil, and only inadvertently serves the cause of good. There is no reason to think that Rowling's inner logic will echo Tolkien's—indeed, that is highly unlikely. It is only those who are using artistic logic—those writers who have consciously imitated Tolkien—who merely echo his deep choices. Rowling may have learned eclectically from all her literary sources, but she is enthralled by none of them. The Harry Potter books have grown from a conscious plan into an unconscious unfolding of a deeply believed inner universe—they have become true art rather than mere planned art—and so Snape, while fulfilling Gollum's literary function, will act out the script that *feels* right to Rowling.

That very fact is actually our key to seeing where Snape's character is going: as we track his progress through the books and see how Rowling uses him, we can discover what he *means* to her as well as what he *does* for the storyline. We may not be able to come up with a definitive answer—after all, Rowling's unconscious logic may contain twists as yet unrevealed to us—but we can still come to conclusions that have the ring of truth to them.

I am not proposing that we psychoanalyze Rowling. Fiction is a poor tool for that. Rather I am proposing that we track Snape's progress through the books to see where she has consciously pointed him, book by book, and where it *seems* she found herself *unconsciously* pointing him. It is only when he becomes a deeply important character to Rowling that he also becomes deeply important to us.

### Snape's Progress

Rowling is on record as saying that she planned all seven volumes from the beginning. But just how detailed was that plan? Did she, in writing volume one, know exactly what she would do with all the characters who were still around in volume seven? I sincerely doubt it, if only because the tone of the series has changed so dramatically—darkening, deepening, and lengthening from volume to volume. Rowling is not now the same writer she was at the beginning, and however detailed her outline was, she would have been hampered, if not shackled, by having to stick to an outline she devised when she was still a relative novice.

It is even possible that her "outline" for the final volume was, in its entirety, "Harry has it out with Voldemort."

And even if she had far more details sketched out for the final volume, I'm willing to bet that as she really got to know the characters by writing about them, she changed her ideas about the roles many of them would play later in the series. It will be interesting, when scholars at last have access not only to the books but also to her working notes at every stage, to see how the creativity that emerges in the writing process transformed her plans for the series.

I have read novels where the author went through the normal process of discovering interesting, unplanned things about his characters—and then reined them in or cut them off so he could fulfill the original outline. Rowling's work shows no signs of such violence having been done to ideas that came up in the process of writing; on the contrary, each volume has been more willing to "learn" from the books before, which almost certainly means that there are many things in the later books that were not in the original outlines—and, quite possibly, things originally planned that will no longer happen, or will mean radically different things when they occur.

So in tracking the way Rowling uses and develops Snape through the six volumes we have at present, I believe we will see a character who becomes far more important to the whole series than he was originally intended to be.

And even if his exact role in the overall series *was* plotted from the start, it is certainly true that he is used very differently from book to book.

## SORCERER'S STONE

In the first volume, Snape's primary role is as decoy. We don't meet him until more than a third of the way through the book—but that's only because Harry doesn't get to Hogwarts 'til then. Everything beforehand serves the function of bringing Harry—and therefore the readers—from the real, modern world into the wizarding world. Throughout those pages, it is almost all comedy, and even when we get to Hogwarts, we have silliness like Dumbledore saying "'a few words. . . . : Nitwit! Blubber! Oddment! Tweak!'" (123).

Indeed, silliness seems to prevail; if Dumbledore had remained the clownish fellow who has everyone sing the school song to whatever melody they choose, it is doubtful many readers would care as much about the series as we do.

In the midst of the silliness, though, Dumbledore does give the warning that signals the beginning of the real story: he warns the students not to go near the "'third-floor corridor on the right-hand side'" unless they "'wish to die a very painful death'" (127).

The very next chapter is entitled "The Potions Master"—like the sixth volume of the series, it is named for Snape. But this is not the Snape of *Half-Blood Prince*. He is harsh, he is unfair, he singles Harry out for negative attention, and he ignores Hermione's competence. (He also takes only a single point from Gryffindor for Harry's "cheek"—in later volumes, point inflation sets in and similar offenses result in ten, then fifty points being deducted.)

Snape's nastiness is necessary to further the plot of this volume: there has to be a red herring, someone Harry and his friends can believe in as the likely villain so that the real perpetrator of evil deeds is not suspected.

Thus Snape gets a lot of pages in the second half of the book. When the real villain is revealed, however, we learn that far from Snape being the villain, he has in fact been acting to protect the school and, on occasion, to save Harry Potter himself.

Why does he do this? Because Harry's father once saved his life. As Dumbledore explains—"dreamily," for Rowling is not yet taking Dumbledore seriously—"'I do believe he worked so hard to protect you this year because he felt that would make him and your father even. Then he could go back to hating your father's memory in peace'" (300).

To me, this is all the evidence I need that Rowling did *not* know the details of Snape's relationship with James Potter when she wrote the first volume. While it is quite believable that Dumbledore would not choose to tell Harry that Snape also felt guilty for having inadvertently provoked Voldemort into killing Harry's parents, it is *not* believable that Dumbledore, knowing the whole story, would "dreamily" say, "Then he could go back to hating your father's memory in peace." It is too light, trivial, and dismissive a thing for Dumbledore to say about Snape, if he (and Rowling) had then known Snape's role as a trusted confederate and former Death Eater responsible for Voldemort hearing of the prophecy that provoked his murder of Harry's parents.

## CHAMBER OF SECRETS

In the second volume, Rowling still is not taking her own fictional world entirely seriously. In the Hogwarts of the later books, it would simply not be believable that Lockhart would be hired in the first place, or that he would remain in his position for more than a few days. Rowling clearly recognized some of these believability problems from the earlier books, as later on she goes to some lengths to give us Dumbledore's justification for keeping Trelawney on the faculty.

Even though *Chamber of Secrets* gets Harry to Hogwarts far more quickly than the first book, there are far fewer references to Snape. That's because his role in the novel is to direct suspicion toward Harry Potter as the person responsible for opening the Chamber, and to serve as comic relief when he is enlisted by Gilderoy Lockhart in the dueling demonstration.

Snape's last appearance in the book is more than seventy pages before the end, when Draco suggests that Snape ought to be made headmaster to replace the suspended Dumbledore. Snape's reaction to this is to reassure Draco that Dumbledore will probably be back soon enough, "though he couldn't suppress a thin-lipped smile," and he "smirked as he swept off" (267).

This is *not* the Snape who can hide his thoughts and feelings from Voldemort—rather this is the Snape who is still nothing more than a device to annoy and harass Harry and his friends. *This* version of Snape covets not just the Dark Arts position, but the headmaster's office as well. There is no trace of this sort of trivializing of Snape in the last few volumes.

Before that, we see Snape when Harry and Ron sneak past him under the Invisibility Cloak—and Snape conveniently sneezes so he doesn't hear their passage (259). And before *this* trivial use of Snape, the previous use of him is in the duel where Harry's ability to speak to snakes is revealed (193).

It is clear in *Chamber of Secrets* that Snape is definitely a minor character, only slightly more important than most other professors, and far less important than Hagrid. There is no promise here of what he's going to become. He is merely a caricature left over from the first volume, ready to be trotted out when he is needed . . . to sneeze.

## PRISONER OF AZKABAN

In *Prisoner of Azkaban*, the series takes its first serious turn toward the depth of the later volumes. Sirius Black plays the part that Snape played in the first volume—he's the red herring that seems to be a villain and then turns out to be trying to help Harry. But this time the story centers around Harry discovering more about his father, and the most important character is actually Lupin, who guides Harry through his discoveries that he has the same Patronus as his father and that James Potter was part of a group of four very talented magical pranksters whose games sometimes got out of hand.

When Ron's pathetic rat Scabbers turns out to be the Animagus who actually committed the crimes Sirius Black was convicted of, we see the best example of Rowling taking something very minor from an earlier book and investing it with far more importance. Scabbers is barely present in *Chamber of Secrets*, but as soon as Rowling knows that he matters after all, he's brought back in full force. When Rowling decides a character is going to be important at the climax, she moves him to the forefront—which, with Scabbers, consists of his ongoing struggle with Hermione's cat. What seems like a running gag actually serves to keep us aware of a character who is going to be revealed as a villain in the great "reveal" scene.

Snape is important in this plot, but primarily as a complicating factor. He hates Lupin but still prepares the potion that keeps him from turning wolf at the full moon; yet he also gives very strong hints to the students about what Lupin really is, and it is Snape who provides the last-minute jeopardy, turning Sirius Black over to the authorities and lobbying for his immediate execution.

As with the first volume, Snape's role is important in the immediate plot, but not yet in the long-range story. It's as if Rowling came up with the idea that Snape's life was once saved by James Potter solely to make it believable, in *Sorcerer's Stone*, that someone as malicious as Snape would have been trying to protect Harry after all. Perhaps Rowling thought more about how such a thing could come to be and came up with the details of the foursome who created the Marauder's Map and how James Potter saved him—from a prank that was heading for something really ugly.

Snape remains in this volume as vindictive as ever, but at least now his malice seems more justified. We also begin to see more clearly that he is becoming an ironic figure: as in *Chamber of Secrets*, he constantly catches Harry in the middle of some kind of mischief, but whereas in *Chamber of Secrets* he invariably assigns the worst possible motive to Harry's actions, even when his version is absurdly, obviously wrong, in *Prisoner of Azkaban*, Snape's accusations against Harry are often very accurate. Harry really *is* violating rules, and not trivial ones; Harry really *is* constantly lying; Harry really *is* so arrogant that he thinks he knows better than anyone, and withholds the truth about what he's doing even from Dumbledore.

Thus Snape is moving closer to the center of Rowling's attention. She is using him now, not just as an obstacle (though he still is one), but also as a tool for pointing out Harry's own moral ambiguity. Harry leaps to conclusions; Harry deceives some of the very people he ought to trust most; Harry has contempt for rules even when they exist to protect him and others. Snape's fury at Harry may have begun with the malice that James Potter earned, but it is Harry's own fault that Snape is able to find so very much ammunition to use against him. Rowling is intertwining Snape and Harry in a far more complicated way than before.

## GOBLET OF FIRE

When this fourth volume opens with what amounts to a summary of the story-to-date (which Rowling no longer attempts in the later books), it is significant, I think, that Snape does not even rate a mention. Nothing he has done in the previous books is actually important to understanding what is now happening. But this is the last time that is true.

For even though Snape barely appears in this book, in the scene in the cemetery, where the Death Eaters assemble to watch Voldemort resume his physical body and, they assume, kill Harry Potter, we get our first glimmer of Snape's role as double agent: Voldemort's trusted servant, reporting to him about Hogwarts, and Dumbledore's spy, reporting to him about Voldemort and the Death Eaters. Not that Snape is present— he is only referred to obliquely, and the most obvious reference, the one that *seems* to refer to him, in fact refers to Barty Crouch, who is masquerading as Mad-Eye Moody. (So once again Snape is a red herring, distracting Harry from the *real* enemy.)

The *real* statement of Snape's new role comes when, near the very end of the book, Dumbledore asks Harry and Snape to shake hands as loyal compatriots in the struggle against Voldemort and then turns to Snape and says, "'[Y]ou know what I must ask you to do. If you are ready . . . if you are prepared . . .' Snape turns pale and says, 'I am'"; then he leaves to join Voldemort and pretend to be his loyal servant (713).

Among Snape's few appearances earlier in the book is what is arguably his cruelest moment, when he humiliates Hermione about something she can't help, her personal appearance (300).

It is also in this book that Snape gives his clearest list of complaints about Harry, right to his face: "'To me, Potter, you are nothing but a nasty little boy who considers rules to be beneath him'" (516). Snape accuses Harry of lying, whereupon Harry lies to him repeatedly. Snape is not unjustified when he threatens Harry with Veritaserum—and both Harry and the readers understand that if Harry were forced to tell the truth to Snape, the truth would *not* vindicate Harry the way it would have in *Chamber of Secrets*.

For the first time in the series, the reader can't help but recognize that Snape has a point. For the first time, Harry's shenanigans are seriously questioned—and Snape does the questioning. This is how Rowling prepares us to see Snape as being something other than malicious, and we are not appalled or incredulous when Dumbledore trusts Snape with his mission among the Death Eaters.

## ORDER OF THE PHOENIX

Snape's new role in the story—as the member of the Order of the Phoenix who is fulfilling the most dangerous assignment of all (at the moment, at least)—actually keeps him out of the book for a long time. He shows up briefly on page sixty-nine, where the kids talk about how much they loathe him, and then surfaces again only as Potions Master at Hogwarts, where he evanesces a potion that Harry did, in fact, botch (232–234). It's annoying, but not as vicious as things Snape has done in the past. He shows up again on page 309, again merely as a teacher.

Why is he so invisible? Because Dolores Umbridge is filling the role of persecutor now, providing a powerful contrast with the relatively mild punishments Snape inflicts. The contrast is, I think, deliberate: Rowling is rehabilitating Snape a little, making him seem better than before because Umbridge is so much worse—and for so little reason. Snape, at least, had some justification for resenting Harry; Umbridge is simply evil.

When, on page 362, we begin Umbridge's visit to Snape's class, we see Snape acting with dignity. Gone are the smirks that afflicted him constantly in the early books. Now his answers are quiet, his expression unfathomable; when his lip curls, it is with impatience at genuine stupidity. He still wipes out Harry's potion yet again and assigns him an extra essay, but now we see him as a man with some self-control, and his punishments as a mere annoyance compared to Umbridge's sadism.

# The Case for Snape's Innocence

On page 400 we catch a glimpse of Snape overbooking the Quidditch field for Slytherin's team, and then don't see him again until he comes to Harry with the news that he is going to teach him Occlumency, at Dumbledore's request.

Then begins a rather intense series of scenes between Harry and Snape, as Harry resists Snape's lessons and Dumbledore's orders (typical of Harry) and does not practice his Occlumency, preferring to keep having his dreams of the room where a great and important secret is being kept. When we finally discover what was really going on with these dreams, we realize that Harry was being suckered by Voldemort, and if he had paid more attention to Snape, things might have turned out better.

Meanwhile, though, we learn considerably more about Snape's character—including through Harry's indecent penetration of Snape's secret memories (639-650). The result of this act is that Snape discontinues the lessons in Occlumency, Harry is appalled at his father's cruelty and rushes to Sirius Black to help with his disillusionment—and the readers now have vastly more sympathy for Snape than ever before.

This is where Snape turns: Rowling has elevated him to a complex character rather than the iconic figure he had been before. We actually care about him as a person, and not just because of what he might do to interfere with Harry's plans. Snape is the hero of his own story now, and we are interested in seeing what becomes of him for his own sake. It is only now that Snape becomes worthy, as a fictional character, of playing the role that is being prepared for him in the final volume.

On page 833, Harry's and Dumbledore's assessments of Snape are patently unfair. After telling Dumbledore that, "'Snape stopped giving me Occlumency lessons! . . . He threw me out of his office!'" He goes on:

> "Snape made it worse, my scar always hurt worse after lessons with him—" Harry remembered Ron's thoughts on the subject and plunged on. "How do you know he wasn't trying to soften me up for Voldemort, make it easier for him to get inside my—"
>
> "I trust Severus Snape," said Dumbledore simply. "But I forgot—another old man's mistake—that some wounds run too deep for the healing. I thought Professor Snape could overcome his feelings about your father—I was wrong."

Harry is grossly unfair—he neglects to point out that Snape threw him out of his office *after* Harry indecently pried into a hidden memory that Snape clearly did not want him to see. And Harry also neglects to point out that even when Snape was teaching him, Harry didn't really try to learn how to blank his mind.

Dumbledore is unfair to answer Harry's wild accusations with the mere assertion that he trusts Snape, followed by an irrelevant statement that seems to throw the blame for the failure of the lessons on Snape alone, because he couldn't "overcome his feelings about" James Potter.

I don't know how many readers reacted to this passage as I did—perhaps most took these statements at face value. But I found myself mentally defending Snape exactly as, in previous books, I mentally defended Harry against Snape's wild accusations. For me, at least, Rowling had succeeded in momentarily transferring my allegiance to Snape.

### HALF-BLOOD PRINCE

Volume six is Snape's book, to put it simply. He is the title character. The volume begins and ends with his actions. Throughout the story, Harry has a close relationship with Snape's younger self through his marginal notes in a Potions book. Thus we learn to experience Snape as a brilliant, creative young wizard—though we don't know it's Snape, of course, until after he has killed Dumbledore.

Ay, there's the rub—Snape kills Harry's sole remaining father figure.

Hermione repeatedly points out to Harry that whatever he learns from the Half-Blood Prince's book, he could have learned just by paying better attention to Snape's lessons right from the start. It becomes perfectly clear to us that if Harry had not been distracted from Snape's teaching by his loathing for the man, he would have become a better wizard.

At the same time, it is hardly Harry's fault that Snape goads him mercilessly before Harry has even had time to do anything wrong. But just as Snape has never gotten over his treatment at the hands of James Potter and friends, so Harry can't get past Snape's malice in order to learn from him. Snape's loathing for James Potter didn't stop Snape from becoming a powerful wizard with skills that, in one area at least, Occlumency, surpassed those of Voldemort. But Harry's loathing of Snape *does* stop him from learning the very things that Snape is uniquely capable of teaching him.

This volume draws Snape upward to the level of Dumbledore in importance to the story. Meanwhile Ron and Hermione become less central—they are shut out of the core story of this volume, serving more as distractions and comic relief. It's as if Rowling has to keep reminding herself to include them, because the energy of the story is now being generated by Harry, Dumbledore, Snape, Draco, and Voldemort himself. Harry's enemies are, in fact, more important to this story than his friends.

But that's partly because this is the first volume whose story doesn't actually end. None of the major problems in this book are resolved—only the relatively trivial problem of the identity of the Half-Blood Prince. Instead of being self-contained, this volume is rather a long first act, setting up the final volume of the series. There are no important new characters introduced; rather, the existing cast is thrust forward into new, more demanding, more mature roles.

And when that happened, Snape came into his own. From the red herring role in the first volume to the complicator, obstacle, and even comic relief he was in the next few, Snape has forced his way into being one of the most complex and interesting characters in the series. He matters now.

Which is why we can be sure that Rowling has no intention of throwing him away. If he is now merely another Death Eater, serving Voldemort faithfully, all that preparation was essentially wasted. We see what happens to Wormtail after his prominent role at the climax of *Prisoner of Azkaban*—once he joins Voldemort, he shows up now and then, but we don't actually *care* about him. Rowling wastes no effort trying to make him into somebody.

Thus Rowling's elevation of Snape into major-character status only makes artistic sense if Snape's actions in the next book are pivotal. And his actions will only be pivotal if they are in doubt. And they will only be in doubt if we are given clear reasons to believe that his killing of Dumbledore might *not* have been the evil action that Harry and his friends assume it to have been.

## Speculations on Character

Another approach to predicting how Snape will act in the final book is to try to understand the traits that dominate his character.

## SNAPE AS SLYTHERIN

Slytherins are not necessarily evil—what typifies them is ambition.

Persons of limited ability can only satisfy their ambition by attaching themselves to someone stronger who will raise them up. Thus ambition leads to slavish loyalty—but to immediate abandonment when the person they have attached to seems to be slipping or failing.

We saw plenty of that during Voldemort's time as one-seventh of a soul, after he "died" from the rebound of his Killing Curse on baby Harry. A few remained loyal, clinging to their faith in Voldemort's supremacy; others denied him immediately, lest they be brought down by his fall.

Slytherins, however, make untrustworthy servants *and* untrustworthy masters. Because they are ambitious, they will resent the one they serve—Voldemort's followers, except perhaps a few demented ones such as Bellatrix—do not love him; on the contrary, they hate him, because they resent him for overshadowing them. Each *wants* to be supreme; it is only because Voldemort exists that their ambition is suppressed.

And Voldemort will also resent everyone who helps him. He wants to stand alone. Once he stands without significant enemies or rivals, he will certainly destroy everyone whose help he depended on to reach that position, because it will be unbearable to him to be in anyone's debt.

Now let's consider Snape as an exemplar of the Slytherin personality. Quite independently of any connection with Voldemort—before he was a Death Eater, in other words—Snape's ambition led him to style himself, albeit privately, as "the Half-Blood Prince." He was brilliant and knew he was brilliant; he created new spells and invented new potions. He learned Occlumency to the degree that he could hide his thoughts from anyone.

No wonder his humiliation during his school days at the hands of Sirius Black and James Potter cannot be forgotten, and colors his response to James's son—especially since one of his unhappiest memories is an occasion when James afflicted him with a spell that Severus Snape himself had invented.

Snape's ambition is more telling when it comes to his relationship with Voldemort. The second-most ambitious wizard in the world will not be Voldemort's *servant*, but his rival. No one will suffer more frustration at Voldemort's supremacy than the person who believes that position is his by right. In fact, it is no accident that Snape's background echoes Voldemort's in being the child of a miserable mating between a cruel Muggle and a lovestruck wizard woman. Both of them loathe "Mudbloods" precisely because they are themselves tainted.

But they are definitely not the same person. Voldemort, in his youthful days as Tom Riddle, had the self-control to make himself seem a model student at Hogwarts—he became Head Boy even as he was already committing murders and creating Horcruxes. He was attractive and gathered followers around him.

Snape, on the other hand, was vain enough not to bother altering his appearance or demeanor in order to seem attractive to others. This might mark him as less ambitious than Voldemort, or it might mark him as being more proud, at least in his youth, for he would not stoop to seek the approval of anyone he did not respect.

What is certain is that if there is anyone among the Slytherins of the wizarding world who would hate, resent, and happily work against Voldemort, it is Snape. If he serves Voldemort, it will be with resentment at having to be subservient. But that is also true if he serves Dumbledore.

Knowing that Voldemort is immortal must be exceptionally galling to an ambitious wizard—Snape knows he will spend his *whole* life subservient to Voldemort, even if Voldemort doesn't eliminate him. His ambition will never, never be satisfied.

So if Slytherin ambition really is the primary key to Snape's character, then he himself has no loyalty to anyone. He hides his feelings from all, and pretends loyalty to both Dumbledore and Voldemort, biding his time. However much Snape hates Harry Potter, he will not allow permanent harm to come to the only person who might have the power to defeat Voldemort.

In this light, it makes perfect sense that Snape sees Harry as weak, careless, vain, grandiose, and not particularly talented. The boy wizard has so far bested, or at least evaded, Voldemort at every encounter, but only because of the magics of other people who protect him. Snape may well believe that if he manages to be present at the deadly final encounter between Harry and Voldemort, then he might be able to turn circumstances toward satisfying his own ambition:

1. If Harry wins, Snape would believe he could certainly kill Harry, having no magical bond with him the way Voldemort has. No linking of wands, no connection of minds through

the scar—Snape can simply finish him off and stand alone in Voldemort's place.

2. If Voldemort wins, but is seriously weakened by the encounter, Snape could strike instantly and fatally, killing Voldemort himself.

3. If Voldemort wins, and is all the stronger for it, then Snape can continue to present himself as Voldemort's loyal servant, and at least survive until he can find some other way to best Voldemort—or until Voldemort eliminates him precisely because he owes him so much.

This view of Snape is not inconsistent with anything Rowling has shown us of the man. This might be precisely how she is planning to use him at the climax of the seventh book.

In that case, we must view Snape as having been a triple agent, deceiving both Dumbledore and Voldemort.

But Rowling will then have the obligation of explaining to us why Dumbledore trusted him so completely.

### SNAPE AS LOVE-STARVED GENIUS

Let's leave in place our assumptions about Snape's ambitions, but now let's suppose that a hunger for love and/or respect is another determining factor in his character.

When Harry cast his *Protego* spell against Snape during an attempt to teach him Occlumency, and was given a rush of Snape's memories, what did he see?

> [A] hook-nosed man was shouting at a cowering woman, while a small dark-haired boy cried in a corner. . . . A greasy-haired teenager sat alone in a dark bedroom, pointing his wand at the ceiling, shooting down flies. . . . A girl was laughing as a scrawny boy tried to mount a bucking broomstick— (*Order of the Phoenix* 591-592).

It is tempting to read into this a profound loneliness—the pride in Snape hates humiliation, but is humiliation perhaps worse in front of women? Or is he merely starved for respect?

Or is it parental love that he needs? Is that what he gets from Dumbledore? Is what he loves about Dumbledore not that Dumbledore is good, but that he shows Snape respect and trust?

Far from being love-starved, however, Snape seems to seek to be alone. When he has the respect and devotion of Draco and his fellow students, Snape definitely favors them—but he is quite capable of being stern with them when he feels like it, and there is scant sign of him sharing intimate friendship with anyone. If he wanted love and respect, he could have dressed to conform while he was a student and offered an occasional smile or sign of warmth; it seems more likely that that particular part of him has been shut down.

## Snape as Surly Good Guy

Maybe Snape secretly loves the Good and loathes Evil. Perhaps this will lead him to save or help Harry Potter, or destroy Voldemort, at the end. Perhaps this is why he has served Dumbledore all along—including, finally, killing him when that formed part of Dumbledore's plan.

By that view, one could see all of Snape's meanness as an act. But it's an act he maintains so consistently, relentlessly, and egregiously that one has to think it's an act that he enjoys—which would mean it isn't an act at all.

Snape is so consistently, needlessly cruel and unfair that he is obviously ruled by malice. There are plenty of examples in his treatment of Harry, but the example that sticks out most is his response when a stray curse has left Hermione with overgrown front teeth. "'I see no difference,'" says Snape, sending her away in tears (*Goblet of Fire* 300). To needlessly hurt a socially powerless child, however annoying she might be, is a cruelty that is hard to explain away.

So maybe he is a good person who is also mean. Doesn't that also describe the way we are expected to view James Potter and Sirius Black? Black is a "good guy" even though he once, as a cruel joke, sent Severus Snape down a tunnel leading to a ravening werewolf—an act of attempted voluntary manslaughter at best.

James Potter knew this was going too far and stopped Snape just in time, saving him—but it was also James Potter who maliciously, for nothing more than his own and Sirius's amusement, dangled Snape upside down, exposing his dirty underwear and skinny body in front of several girls.

If people can behave this way and still be "good guys" in these books (though to my mind, Sirius Black stopped being a good guy as soon as I knew these things about him), then one can only admit that Snape might be a good guy, too.

One can more easily justify Snape's meanness than that of James Potter and Sirius Black. Snape is ashamed of his own ancestry and therefore especially despises "Mudbloods," and Hermione *can* be an annoying know-it-all. As a know-it-all himself you'd think Snape might be a bit kinder; but it's just as logical that what he hates in Hermione is precisely her resemblance to himself, since she is an unattractive (at that point in the series) know-it-all, and so was he—he hates her as he hates those aspects in himself.

Or perhaps he hates her because, despite her brains and Mudblood ancestry and unattractiveness, she has found some very close friends. Perhaps his malicious treatment of her has to do with the fact that *she* was accepted by Harry Potter and became part of his group, while Severus Snape was never accepted by Harry's father, or admitted into *his* group.

As to Snape's malice toward Harry, one can find some justification in Harry's resemblance to his father, his contempt for the rules, and the awe that others hold him in. To Snape, this is simply James Potter all over again—and except for not being anything like the outstanding student his father was, Harry seems to go out of his way to justify Snape's opinion of him.

So, from what we see of Snape's pointlessly malicious actions, he is somewhat more justified than James Potter and Sirius Black ever were in their treatment of him. If we admit them as "good guys," then we certainly cannot rule Snape out, at least not on that basis alone.[2] We have seen Snape's malice and vindictiveness, but what we never see from him is actual evil. When Snape punishes Harry, it is usually for genuine offenses, and if the punishment seems excessive, it is never actually cruel. In case we miss the point, Dolores Umbridge's vicious physical punishment of Harry during detention shows us what a truly evil person might do with a position of absolute power over an annoying child.

---

[2] It was fine that Sirius and Lupin both repented their bad acts toward Snape, having learned to be better people. But their cruelty to him arose out of their nature, and not out of any harm Snape had done them, while Snape has genuine grievances against them, and damage done to him in adolescence does not evaporate just because the perpetrators later regretted what they did. To say he should have gotten over it is to hold him to a higher standard than most people are able to achieve.

# The Case for Snape's Innocence

The line between meanness and evil seems to be clearly drawn in the moral universe of the Harry Potter series. As Bellatrix says to Harry when he casts the Cruciatus Curse on her in the Ministry of Magic: "'Never used an Unforgivable Curse before, have you, boy?' she yelled. . . . 'You need to *mean* them, Potter! You need to really want to cause pain-to enjoy it—righteous anger won't hurt me for long—I'll show you how it is done, shall I? I'll give you a lesson—'" (*Order of the Phoenix* 810).

We know Bellatrix is evil—she drove Neville's parents insane with the Cruciatus and took pleasure from it. And that is the dividing line, where ambition and pride cross over into true evil—that the death and suffering of others become ends in themselves rather than merely means to an end. This is what marked Voldemort from the start, even before he came to Hogwarts as Tom Riddle. He was a torturer simply for the pleasure of it; when he killed, he took trophies, because they were occasions he wanted to remember.

This is also the dividing line for Draco Malfoy. He thinks he is very bad, and he has attempted to cast Unforgivable Curses before. But his feeble attempts to murder Dumbledore—the cursed necklace, the poisoned bottle of mead—show his reluctance to do such a deed: it has to be kept at a remove. When he stands before his intended victim, face to face, he cannot bring himself to do it.

Draco is malicious, but he has not surrendered his human dread of murder; he has kept shreds of decency that, in that moment, trip him up. And this is so even though it would be a murder, not simply out of malice, but required in order to save his own life and the lives of his parents. People who are far from evil have chosen to kill under such circumstances. Yet he cannot do it. Therefore he is still redeemable.

Consider Snape in this light, and we have no conclusive evidence that he has ever crossed the line into true evil. Not that other characters in the books would agree with that statement. When Harry is discussing Snape's killing of Dumbledore with other members of the Order of the Phoenix, he says:

"Snape passed Voldemort the information that made Voldemort hunt down my mum and dad. Then Snape told Dumbledore he hadn't realized what he was doing, he was really sorry he'd done it, sorry that they were dead."

They all stared at him.

"And Dumbledore believed that?" said Lupin incredulously. "Dumbledore believed Snape was sorry James was dead? Snape *hated* James" (*Half-Blood Prince* 616).

Nobody in the room argues with Lupin's statement, but Harry himself should have known better than to regard that as a serious answer. Remember that Snape felt a debt to James Potter for having kept him from dying at the hands of a werewolf (Lupin himself, ironically, as recounted in *Prisoner of Azkaban*), and repaid the debt by repeatedly saving Harry from Quirrell's attempts to kill him in *Sorcerer's Stone*. If Snape felt he owed that debt to James Potter, is it likely he would deliberately have provided Voldemort with information that would provoke him to murder James and Lily? And even if we suppose that Snape actually felt indebted partly *because* he indirectly caused James's and Lily's deaths, that *still* contradicts Lupin's opinion that it was impossible that Snape could be sorry James was dead.

In fact, the whole scene on pages 615 and 616 of *Half-Blood Prince* consists of people talking each other into a firm belief that Snape had always been deceiving Dumbledore, with no one advancing the possibility that just as Harry had done awful things to Dumbledore *at Dumbledore's command*, Snape might have killed him for the same reason. It is hardly surprising that they are unable to make that mental leap, partly because Dumbledore is so newly dead, and partly because they all dislike, despise, or resent Snape for their own reasons. It seems to them so much likelier that Snape, a reformed Death Eater, was actually a double agent who had been deceiving even Dumbledore, than that Dumbledore's murder at Snape's hand had been planned from the time that Draco Malfoy was assigned to do the murder.

For that is the only viable alternative explanation for Snape's killing of Dumbledore. When, near the beginning of *Half-Blood Prince*, Snape takes the Unbreakable Vow to kill Dumbledore himself if Draco could not do it (36–37), it can be taken at face value, or it can be taken as something Snape agrees to do only because he already knows that it is part of Dumbledore's plan to die.

We can speculate about why Dumbledore might plan such a thing, whether or not he is going to be resurrected. Perhaps he thought that if Voldemort fully believed that Dumbledore was dead, he would act carelessly and prematurely, underestimating the power that resided in Harry because of the purity of the love inside him and all the bonds of love that surround him. Perhaps he thought that as long as Harry believed Dumbledore would always bail him out in a crisis, Harry would not prepare himself as intensely as he should for the inevitable confrontation with Voldemort.

## Evidence

The only evidence I'm aware of that Snape might have been assigned by Dumbledore to make that Unbreakable Vow and then act on it, killing him on the tower, is deliberately inconclusive. It comes from a conversation between Dumbledore and Snape that is overheard by Hagrid, who reluctantly tells Harry about it. Rowling could hardly have made the report more unreliable and less conclusive: Hagrid isn't the best witness, and his telling is distorted by his own desire to minimize the importance of what he has heard:

> "Well—I jus' heard Snape sayin' Dumbledore took too much fer granted an' maybe he—Snape—didn' wan' ter to it anymore—"
> "Do what?"
> "I dunno, Harry, it sounded like Snape was feelin' a bit overworked, tha's all—anyway, Dumbledore told him flat out he'd agreed ter do it an' that was all there was to it. Pretty firm with him. An' then he said summat abou' Snape makin' investigations in his House, in Slytherin" (*Half-Blood Prince* 405–406).

Hagrid has his own lame theory about what this conversation might have meant, but it's obvious nonsense. We readers, though, who know about Snape's Unbreakable Vow to protect Draco and kill Dumbledore if Draco failed to carry out the assignment, can easily see that what Hagrid overheard *might* have been Snape's insistence that he did not want to carry out the plan to kill Dumbledore, and Dumbledore reminding him that he must do it or die himself. The sentence "You took an Unbreakable Vow" is just the sort of thing that Hagrid might repeat as

"Dumbledore told him flat out he'd agreed ter do it an' that was all there was to it."

And the need for Snape to investigate Slytherin House may have been because Snape had to figure out, without Draco telling him directly, just what his plan for killing Dumbledore *was*. The fact that Snape did *not* know it nearly kept him from being in the right place at the right time to fulfill the terms of his Unbreakable Vow and kill Dumbledore.

If this is not the meaning of what Hagrid overhears, then what else can it have been?

After Dumbledore is dead, Harry Potter never thinks of or speaks about what Hagrid overheard. In effect, Rowling drops this information into the middle of a nice thick book, nearly 400 pages after the taking of the Unbreakable Vow and nearly 200 pages before the event that the conversation might have anticipated, and none of the characters give it great significance or bring it up when it might provide an alternate explanation for Snape's behavior. Rowling has played fair with us, she has tipped her hand, but only for a brief moment, in a blur, expecting us to forget it as thoroughly as Harry does, because Hagrid's telling is so confusing that we never hear directly what was actually said.

If the words "Unbreakable Vow" had been said at that point, we would have remembered, and we would know that Snape was trying to get out of killing Dumbledore. The conversation that Hagrid overheard was, in effect, Snape's equivalent of saying, "Let this cup pass from me; nevertheless, thy will, not mine, be done" (Matthew 26:39).

In light of that conversation, I believe that we can actually be quite sure that Snape, in killing Dumbledore, is doing his will, exactly as Harry does Dumbledore's will by forcing him to drink all the liquid in the cave, which is what weakens Dumbledore so much that he can hardly stand when Draco faces him. Obeying Dumbledore tests the moral fiber of his dearest friends—they have to choose between doing good (i.e., not killing people, not forcing them to drink slow-acting poisons) and being loyal and obedient to him.

### What Will Snape Do Now?

Knowing that it was Dumbledore's will that Snape kill him does *not* tell us much about what Snape will do in the next book. Like Gollum, he is still unpredictable.

After all, Rowling goes to great pains in *Half-Blood Prince* to show us that Dumbledore is not always right. The locket he nearly dies to obtain is not one of Voldemort's four missing Horcruxes; he makes other mistakes and admits them. He might have counted on Snape's continuing to obey him and follow his plans after killing him, but will he?

Snape certainly knew Dumbledore's plan up to the point of killing him—but did he know *anything* about what Dumbledore intended to do (or have someone else do) after he was dead? Though Snape is a gifted Occlumens, that does not mean that Voldemort will *never* be able to penetrate Snape's mind; therefore it is most likely Dumbledore told Snape nothing more than Snape needed to know.

Thus Snape may now feel himself to be a free agent. Even if he would gladly continue to help Dumbledore accomplish his purposes, he can't do much if he doesn't know what Dumbledore's plans are. He may even conclude that whatever Dumbledore's plan was, it must have failed, and now Snape must make his own accommodation with Voldemort . . . or wait for whatever opportunity presents itself, as I suggested before.

What we do know is this: In Snape's last contacts with Harry, he repeatedly saves the boy he despises so much, and gives him advice that is undoubtedly going to be crucial to Harry surviving or prevailing in his final confrontation with Voldemort. Harry must learn to hide his thoughts and cast spells without speaking them aloud or even thinking them in such a way that the "'most accomplished Legilimens the world has ever seen'" would be able to detect them (*Half-Blood Prince* 26).

In *Harry Potter and the Half-Blood Prince*, Snape is the title character; his vow at the beginning and his murder of Dumbledore near the end frame the story; the book he annotated succeeds in doing what Snape himself could never do in person—teach Harry to be an accomplished potion-maker. One can argue that despite all distractions, the sixth volume of the series is *about* Snape.

It is highly unlikely that Rowling would do all this if Snape were not to be important in the final book. Rowling has carefully avoided letting us know, with certainty, just what motivates Snape's actions, but she has also kept Snape from ever crossing the line into evil. Thus we will, in all likelihood, come to the climax of the final book not knowing what Snape will do in the moment of crisis.

My own prediction is that Snape will reveal himself to be as loyal to Dumbledore as Harry Potter himself; in fact, I go further, and offer the thought that Rowling will have Snape give his life in the process of help-ing Harry Potter prevail in the final battle. There are several reasons I believe this—though I suspect one of the major ones is simply that that is how I, as a novelist myself, would use the character of Snape.

My other reasons for believing this are simple enough:

1. Rowling has built him up so much, in the fifth and sixth vol-umes, that she must be planning for him to play a major role in the climax of the series.

2. Rowling has laid the groundwork (in Hagrid's report of the overheard conversation) for revealing to Harry that Snape has been loyal to Dumbledore all along.

3. By having Dumbledore refuse to explain his reason for trust-ing Snape, Rowling has, in effect, promised us that we will find out the reason, and that it will be far more convincing than the lame reasons the Order of the Phoenix speculates about at the end of *Half-Blood Prince*.

4. There is no other character whose sacrifice would be so pow-erful *and* acceptable to readers. Of course she could have Ron or Hermione or Ginny sacrifice him- or herself, but they've all been in jeopardy before, and acted nobly, and I think Rowling has no desire to torment her loyal readers like that. As for Harry dying in the process of killing Voldemort—well, she could do that, but she won't enjoy going through the rest of her life without a single literate person ever speaking to her again.

   And aside from those four, there is no character whose noble death would mean as much as Snape's, once his loyalty is revealed. Rowling has set him up for sacrifice.

5. Rowling has made Snape so malicious, so unfair, so vindic-tive, so cruel to Harry and his friends over the course of the first six volumes that, even though we have been given some justifications for his actions, it would be very difficult for her to bring him through the final confrontation alive—for she

would then have the problem of deciding how Snape and Harry will treat each other after Snape behaves nobly.

What is she going to do, have Snape wash his hair and, now that he doesn't have to act so bad, give Harry a big old hug and say, "I knew you could do it, Harry, my lad!"?

Not that there wouldn't be a precedent: at the end of the Star Wars trilogy, George Lucas shows us Darth Vader, a mass murderer and war criminal, so completely redeemed by the act of saving Luke's life that his soul appears as the moral equal of Yoda and Obi-Wan when they all appear to Luke at the Ewok sock hop.

If Lucas can get away with such an absurd moral turnaround, I suppose Rowling can make Snape be nice—or maybe have him still be a bit snippy but good-at-heart. I think Rowling has more integrity as an artist than Lucas, however, and we'll see no such nonsense. If Snape does live, he will still be Snape. But I think he will not live.

Snape's offering himself as a noble sacrifice, to save the world from Voldemort and, more specifically, to save the life of the undeserving (in his view) son of one enemy and godson of another, would satisfy Snape's ambition for greatness and recognition and honor. His name would go down in history as one of the greatest of wizards. It's the only motive that would get a Slytherin to act so nobly—but for that very reason it is true to Snape's character.

Like Gollum in Lord of the Rings, Snape is not the character we are rooting for, but he may be the character whose moral struggle means the most to us in the end. And if, like Gollum, Snape dies in the process of bringing down the Dark Lord, we will feel, not pleasure in Snape's downfall, but a wistful longing that things might have turned out differently for him.

# THE GREAT
# SNAPE
# DEBATE

The Harry Potter books are supposed to be about Harry Potter. So why can't we stop talking about Severus Snape?

Love him or love to hate him, Snape has become *the* pivotal character in the Harry Potter series. *Half-Blood Prince* ended with Snape killing Dumbledore—and yet there are plenty of fans who still think the greasy git is innocent. So is Snape on Harry's side, or is he on Voldemort's? Is he bad to the bone, or just misunderstood?

Only after *Deathly Hallows* will we know for sure . . . but we can make some educated guesses now. In *The Great Snape Debate*, you'll get all the facts on Snape's misdeeds so you can decide for yourself. . . .

*The Case*
*for*
*Snape's*
*Guilt*

# THE GREAT
# SNAPE
# DEBATE

*Is Snape Harry Potter's Foe?*

AMY BERNER
JOYCE MILLMAN

exclusive

# The Case for Snape's Guilt

*(For the Case for Snape's Innocence, flip over this book.)*

# I.
# THE CASE FOR
# SNAPE'S GUILT

SEVERUS SNAPE, WHETHER GOOD OR EVIL, fascinates us. His enigmatic nature makes him an intriguing subject, so intriguing that many readers love him, even as he insults and mistreats our hero, Harry. If a character enthralls us, we naturally want him to be someone who we can root for.

But while Snape may still appear to be a riddle, enough evidence exists to suggest that any remaining hopes of him being a "good" character will be dashed in the seventh and final book of the series, *Deathly Hallows*. Despite Dumbledore's assurances throughout six books that Snape is on the officially "good" side of the Potterverse, the side that opposes Lord Voldemort, the reverse is more likely to be true. In spite of what Albus Dumbledore believed, Snape supports Voldemort.

A childhood filled with neglect, first by his parents and then by teachers, made Snape a loner, ripe for torment by his fellow students. But while he might have risen above all that, a horrible temper and a tendency toward holding grudges and seeking vengeance prevented him from doing so. Snape's history and temperament form a foundation that far better supports an evil, self-serving nature than a good one, and Snape has followed that nature with remarkable consistency.

## Part I: The Potterverse Evidence

But you must not forget that Snape was a Death Eater. He will have seen things that. . . . Why do you love him? Why do people love Snape? I do not understand this.
— J. K. ROWLING, Edinburgh Book Festival, 2004

### Snape the Death Eater

"Ever since I found out Snape was teaching here, I've wondered why Dumbledore hired him. Snape's always been fascinated by the Dark Arts, he was famous for it at school. Slimy, oily, greasy-haired kid, he was. . . . Snape knew more curses when he arrived at school than half the kids in seventh year, and he was part of a gang of Slytherins who nearly all turned out to be Death Eaters. . . . Snape's certainly clever and cunning enough to keep himself out of trouble."
— SIRIUS BLACK, *Goblet of Fire* (531)

Severus Snape was a Death Eater and devoted follower of Lord Voldemort, which is the most basic definition of evil in the world of Harry Potter. Those who follow Voldemort are evil, and those who fight against him are good. What possible reason would there be for a loyal Death Eater to turn on one of the most powerful wizards in history? Why would he choose to turn on the only people who had ever accepted him? What could such actions possibly gain him? Snape has every reason to remain loyal to the Death Eaters.

The only logical conclusion is that, in fact, he has. Even while at Hogwarts, he calls Voldemort by the title "the Dark Lord," revealing his deep-seated loyalty. He is always respectful toward Voldemort, far more so than any enemy would or should be. And while this could be explained away as part of his cover *after* the events of *Goblet of Fire*, it does not explain his use of "Dark Lord" in reference to Voldemort in the previous books—particularly before the first hints of Voldemort's return at the end of *Sorcerer's Stone*.

From what Harry observed from Snape's memories, we can surmise that Snape's father was neglectful, cruel, and most likely abusive during his childhood. Then, at Hogwarts, he became the prey of bullies, the victim of pranks by James Potter and his group of friends. It was likely Voldemort, a fellow half-blood wizard, who became Snape's first true father figure. He gave Snape a place where he belonged, a place in which he was welcome for the first time in his life.

Snape would have realized early which group he preferred. Children associate feelings and attitudes with certain groups based on how those groups affect them directly, and those associations often carry on long into adulthood. The young Snape was teased, taunted, and terrorized by boys from Gryffindor, many of whom aligned with the Order of the Phoenix against Voldemort. Those who would be the most likely to talk to him, accept him, and influence him, like Lucius Malfoy, the Lestrange brothers, and the Black sisters, sided with the Death Eaters. Snape would naturally side with the latter.

When Snape originally made the choice to be a Death Eater, he made that choice without the intention of spying for either side. He would have chosen to serve Voldemort because that was where he belonged. He had a kinship with Voldemort that few of his fellow Death Eaters could understand: a half-blood lineage that in no way limited their power. Also, like Voldemort, Snape suffers from a glorified sense of self; as Tom

Riddle styled himself Lord Voldemort during his time at Hogwarts, the young Snape referred to himself as the Half-Blood Prince, a clever, egocentric title. He is ambitious and very intelligent and, as a Slytherin, fully aware of the limitations of selfless pursuits.

Snape is not only a Slytherin, but the (now-former) head of their House, and Slytherins are opportunistic, using their abilities to serve their own interests first and foremost. In seeing the Dark Lord's strength rising, both the first and second time, Snape would be far more likely to choose the side of the fight most likely to bring him power. Even better if that side utilized the Dark Arts, a category of magic of which Snape has been fond since early childhood; after all, we hear repeatedly—from Sirius Black, from every account of his past history; it's clear too from the notes he made in his old Potions book—of his long fascination with the Dark Arts.

Snape's efforts on the side of the Death Eaters have yielded many results; after all, it was Snape himself who overheard Sybil Trelawney's prophecy about the Dark Lord, the one who drove Voldemort to murder Harry's parents and attempt to kill Harry in the first place, the toweringly evil act that set the stage for the entire series.

## Dumbledore's Folly

> Immense brainpower does not protect you from emotional mistakes and I think Dumbledore really exemplifies that. In fact, I would tend to think that being very, very intelligent might create some problems and it has done for Dumbledore, because his wisdom has isolated him, and I think you can see that in the books, because where is his equal, where is his confidante, where is his partner? He has none of those things.
>
> —J. K. ROWLING, MuggleNet/The Leaky Cauldron interview, 2005

> "[Snape] used to be a Death Eater," said Ron stubbornly. "And we've never seen proof that he *really* swapped sides. . . ."
>
> "Dumbledore trusts him," Hermione repeated. "And if we can't trust Dumbledore, we can't trust anyone."
>
> —*Order of the Phoenix* (555)

Can Harry trust Dumbledore's judgment? Not as much as we would like to think. Dumbledore's trust carries a great deal of weight, and that alone had been enough to prove to many characters that Snape is on their side. However, Dumbledore has a habit of believing the best of people, even when evidence suggests that he should not, and forgiving too easily. His beliefs, too, are not always correct. Dumbledore has admitted mistakes in judgment in every book in the series. The *only* reason the Hogwarts staff and the members of the Order of the Phoenix trusted Snape was because Dumbledore trusted him. Was Dumbledore's trust in Snape yet another mistake? Even Rowling herself has publicly agreed that Dumbledore can be trusting to the point of recklessness.

Voldemort has always known about this weakness in Dumbledore, and he knows how to exploit it as well. In *Goblet of Fire*, we read, "'Course Dumbledore trusts you,' growled Moody. 'He's a trusting man, isn't he? Believes in second chances. But me—I say there are spots that don't come off, Snape. Spots that never come off, d'you know what I mean?'"(472). Note that the man speaking here is actually Barty Crouch, Jr., a Death Eater in disguise as Moody, not Mad-Eye Moody himself. It's a clue that Voldemort and the Death Eaters understand how to manipulate Dumbledore—and are also well aware of where Snape's true allegiance lies.

Dumbledore believed that Snape switched sides all those years ago because of his remorse about his role in the Potters' death. However, if Snape was truly remorseful about that crime, so much so that he supposedly risked his life to turn on Voldemort, why was his "worst memory" being humiliated as a student by James Potter instead of the thing that made Snape feel so horrible he risked his life to change sides, James's death? Snape's hatred of James Potter endured despite Snape having indirectly caused his murder, so Dumbledore's primary reason for trusting Snape—the sincerity of Snape's remorse—already seems to be in question.

Dumbledore is not exactly the best judge of character. After all, Dumbledore is the man who brought Tom Riddle to Hogwarts in the first place. Dumbledore knew from their first meeting that Riddle used his power to be cruel and controlling, and while the future Voldemort certainly needed schooling to rein in his power, it should have been apparent from the first that Riddle needed to be supervised more closely than Dumbledore alone could manage. Dumbledore, however, kept what he

knew of Riddle to himself, and thus did not ensure that Riddle was well-watched. If he had, "Lord Voldemort" might never have existed, much less been allowed to come to power.

Dumbledore is far from all-knowing: as headmaster he had no idea that James, Sirius, and Peter had all become Animagi while at Hogwarts, in support of werewolf Remus Lupin. Mere students were able to hide this from him right under his nose, despite needing years to master this difficult skill. James, who led a gang of bullies, also went on to become Head Boy, even though his regular detentions didn't exactly make him a role model.

Dumbledore believed, as did everyone else, that it was Sirius who betrayed James and Lily and that Peter Pettigrew had met an honorable death facing him, despite having known them all as students. It should have been clear that both of these actions went against their natures. But Dumbledore did not trust Sirius enough to be comfortable with him becoming the Potters' Secret-Keeper when they went into hiding, asking to take on that job himself, and he never suspected Peter Pettigrew of being the real traitor. Nor did he detect Scabbers's true identity; even Crookshanks seemed to know that Scabbers was more than he appeared before Dumbledore did.

As headmaster, his responsibility included hiring good teachers that would effectively educate his students, but Dumbledore has hired many teachers that were simply dreadful, including Trelawney, who, though she has two very important prophecies to her name, has no recollection of either of them and even less ability to instruct others in making their own. Even Hermione couldn't stand her. He also hires the terribly boring ghost of Professor Binns, who repeats lectures by rote; Hagrid, who really doesn't have the training to be a teacher no matter how good and loyal he is; and Snape himself, a terrible teacher whether the subject is Potions or Defense Against the Dark Arts.

Firenze, the centaur Dumbledore brought in to take over Divination classes, is a failure as a teacher. He means well as an instructor, and is certainly an improvement over Trelawney, but his ambiguous teaching methods do not adequately communicate his ideas to his human students, making his classes nearly worthless. Sadly, Firenze is cast out of the centaur herd for agreeing to Dumbledore's request to join the teaching staff, ruining any sort of future he could have with his people. Did Dumbledore not realize what would happen to Firenze?

If Dumbledore trusted Snape as implicitly as he claimed, why not give him the Defense Against the Dark Arts teaching position? Even Snape himself admitted that Dumbledore feared that he might relapse and return to his Dark ways. Why would Dumbledore endanger the lives of the students by hiring someone he believed could so easily become a danger to his students? Dumbledore's responsibilities include not only the education of the students in his care, but their safety. For that reason alone, Snape's past should make him unsuitable for *any* post at Hogwarts. Would any of us Muggles allow a murderer, no matter how reformed, to teach our children? Of course not.

Most of the single-year teachers have been even worse; Remus Lupin has been the only one with any merit. (Horace Slughorn appears to be decent so far as well, but he had prior Hogwarts experience.) Dumbledore hires the inept egomaniac Gilderoy Lockhart for the Defense Against the Dark Arts position in Harry's second year, while Harry and his friends see through his thin façade of talent after a single class, despite the fame and reputation that preceded him. Lockhart, however, is not in league with Voldemort, making him an almost decent choice in comparison to some of the others.

Professor Quirrell brings Voldemort himself inside Hogwarts underneath his turban during Harry's first year, but Dumbledore never suspects that the Dark Lord is possessing a faculty member right under his nose. Of all people, Dumbledore should have been able to detect the Dark Lord's presence. He also fails to detect both the danger of the diary Harry finds in his second year and its connection to the teenage Voldemort.

Dumbledore misses yet another Voldemort-sent faculty intruder in Harry's fourth year. Although Dumbledore had known Alastor "Mad-Eye" Moody for years and fought by his side, Barty Crouch, Jr., completely fools Dumbledore when he masquerades in the Auror's place for the entire school year. Dumbledore even works closely with him on the Triwizard Tournament, in addition to overseeing his position as the Defense Against the Dark Arts teacher. If Dumbledore is indeed an accomplished Legilimens as reported, how could he have missed this switch?

The following year, rather than hiring a new Defense Against the Dark Arts professor, he allows the Ministry of Magic to install its own representative, Dolores Umbridge. He is heavily occupied with Order business,

of course, but no matter how busy he may have been, Dumbledore's hands-off approach to this school year leads to disastrous results: students dropping out of school, and his own (temporary) dismissal as well as that of some members of his staff.

Dumbledore's errors in judgment extend far beyond faculty hiring decisions. He and Hagrid station Fluffy, the dangerous Cerberus-like three-headed dog, in an area that any first-year student can access. Not only that, but the "well-protected" Sorcerer's Stone is blocked by a set of creatures and tasks that three mere first-year students are able to overcome all by themselves.

The headmaster also quietly accepts that Harry should compete in the Triwizard Tournament as a fourth wizard "Champion" despite the fact that Harry both did not submit his name into the Goblet of Fire and according to the rules was too young to compete, a fact which should have stopped his name from even entering the Goblet. How could Dumbledore not realize that foul play was involved? Dumbledore's inaction regarding Harry's participation in the Tournament leads to the boy's unwilling participation in Voldemort's return and the tragic death of Cedric Diggory.

After living through that ordeal, Harry needs his mentor for support and guidance, but Dumbledore provides neither. He doesn't even communicate with the increasingly resentful and confused Harry about the Order of the Phoenix and the plans against Voldemort, keeping him at arms' length in order to "protect" him.

That school year, Dumbledore appoints Snape to give Harry lessons in Occlumency so that the boy can learn to shield his mind. But instead of shielding his mind, Snape's lessons seem to open his mind even further to Voldemort's intrusions, laying the foundation for Voldemort's trap at the Ministry. Using a false vision of Sirius in danger, Voldemort lures Harry to the Department of Mysteries, where he hopes Harry will lead them to Trelawney's prophecy. Harry and his friends fall into the trap and become the prey of the waiting Death Eaters, beginning a battle that leads to Sirius's death.

Dumbledore's mistakes have caused harm to himself as well as others. At the beginning of *Half-Blood Prince*, we discover that Dumbledore is not invincible, as evidenced by his withered arm. This is a physical reminder that Dumbledore can indeed be vulnerable and weak. Later, thinking that it was the only way to retrieve a Horcrux, Dumbledore

drank a poisonous potion, only to find that the particular Horcrux he thought lay at its bottom had already been taken by someone else. That blunder, of course, leads directly to his death—he faces Draco and Snape at the top of the tower in a weakened state from the poison in his body.

Is Dumbledore truly a legendary wizard on the order of a Gandalf or a Merlin, as we have been led to believe? His appearance is certainly similar, with his long white beard and robes, but looks can sometimes be deceiving.

There are too many questions about how the rest of the community treats him to be certain that he is fully deserving of his acclaim. While he was awarded the Order of Merlin, First Class, for Grand Sorcery, many of his contemporaries don't seem to think that he is quite as fantastic as those at Hogwarts do.

Although the entire wizarding community fears Voldemort, going so far as to call him "He Who Shall Not Be Named" rather than utter his name, the actual anti-Voldemort response is minor when he returns. Considering Voldemort's past actions, one would think that the threat of his taking power again would be enough to mobilize the entire community. Why do so few witches and wizards believe Dumbledore's claim that Voldemort has returned? Why, despite his lofty position, awards, titles, and experience, are his claims so easily dismissed? Why is Dumbledore's faction so small? Are we really to believe that the community at large is that short-sighted? Perhaps Dumbledore has made other claims that have proved unfounded. Or, perhaps, at Hogwarts, his reputation has been inflated in an effort to keep students in awe of him, therefore encouraging better behavior.

We are told that Dumbledore could have been Minister of Magic and that he was asked three times to take the job. As it could have helped the cause against Voldemort, both in past years and in the current situation, why wouldn't he take the job? As someone who seems to relish other leadership roles, this step would seem natural.

But he is removed from those other leadership positions—Chief Warlock of the Wizengamot and Supreme Mugwump of the International Confederation of Wizards—during his conflict with the British Ministry of Magic under Cornelius Fudge. He is reinstated when the Ministry is forced to concede that he had been correct about Voldemort's return. But is his claim regarding Voldemort really the *only* reason for those dismissals, or could there have been past instances of

errors, of Dumbledore "crying wolf," that set this up? Do Fudge and Dolores Umbridge have enough support to send Dumbledore to Azkaban as they try to do in *Order of the Phoenix*? There are always two sides to every story, and we only know Dumbledore's side. Fudge isn't the brightest wizard, certainly, but his power can only extend so far. Is Dumbledore, with his reputation, experience, position, power, and awards, really *that* politically weak? Apparently so, according to the evidence. But as we see this world through Harry's eyes, we may never fully understand why.

On occasion, Dumbledore admits his mistakes to Harry: believing that Snape could overcome his old hatred of James, keeping Harry in the dark during his fifth year. But most of the time, we forget that the biggest mistakes in each of the books belong to Dumbledore, something that he himself admits: "'I make mistakes like the next man. In fact, being—forgive me—rather cleverer than most men, my mistakes tend to be correspondingly huger'" (*Half-Blood Prince* 197).

### Spinner's End

Although readers have been repeatedly reassured of Snape's loyalty to Dumbledore, all of the supposed "evidence" we have been given is flipped on its head in the second chapter of *Half-Blood Prince*, "Spinner's End." After we witness his conversation with Narcissa Malfoy and Bellatrix Lestrange at his home, it becomes all too apparent that Snape could just as easily be loyal to Voldemort as to Dumbledore. We normally see the wizarding world through Harry's eyes, but for this chapter, that filter is removed, providing the reader with vital information that Harry doesn't have. We can finally see this part of his world clearly, and what we see is as close to a "confession" as Snape has ever given. After reading this chapter in *Half-Blood Prince*, how can any reader be absolutely sure of where Snape's loyalties lie? Each and every one of his self-incriminating explanations to the fanatical Bellatrix both fits the facts and is completely reasonable and believable. Finally, Snape's actions through the years make sense.

Let's look at the explanations one at a time. When Bellatrix asks where he was when the Dark Lord fell, Snape answers that he was at Hogwarts, right where Voldemort had ordered him to be. His task at the time was to spy on Voldemort's primary enemy: Dumbledore. At the time

of Voldemort's defeat, the headmaster believed that Snape was actually a double agent on his behalf, but considering that Snape first came to him about a teaching position at Hogwarts *before* Voldemort was defeated, it is completely plausible that Snape was still working for his Dark Lord when he gained the position at Hogwarts, and had simply altered his method of obtaining it. Snape went to Hogwarts with Voldemort's permission and blessing. The plan to use Snape as a spy against the opposition was Voldemort's idea first, not Dumbledore's.

Bellatrix then asks why Snape never made any attempt to find Voldemort when he vanished. Snape responds that he thought that his master had been utterly vanquished. Considering that most other Death Eaters thought so as well, including the ever-faithful Lucius Malfoy, this answer is completely reasonable. Why would he risk his own safety for a leader he thought to be not only defeated but deceased?

When asked what he had been doing all the years since, living "'in Dumbledore's pocket'" (25), Snape claims that the Dark Lord is pleased that he never deserted his assigned post. Because of Snape, Voldemort has a line into his enemy's stronghold immediately upon returning to power. And aside from all that remaining at Hogwarts did for Voldemort, look at all that it did for Snape. He had a respectable, comfortable job as head of Slytherin and Potions Master at Hogwarts; he remained under the protection of the Chief Warlock of the Wizengamot, Dumbledore, who defended him and saved him from imprisonment in Azkaban; and he held on to the hope that he might one day teach young wizards and witches about his beloved Dark Arts. As a true Slytherin, out above all for his own personal gain and always primed to take any opportunity that presented itself, why would he have left such a comfortable position, regardless of loyalties, to honor the memory of a master who was no longer alive?

The next question Bellatrix poses is about the reason Snape stopped Voldemort from procuring the Sorcerer's Stone. Snape points out that he had no idea that Voldemort had possessed Professor Quirrell; he thwarted Quirrell because Quirrell was "'unworthy'" of the Stone (28). And how could Snape have known? Even Dumbledore was fooled, never realizing that Voldemort lived under his own roof within the meek and feeble Quirrell. Snape's disdain for him isn't a surprise, given the other man's demeanor. And the fact that Quirrell held what Snape no doubt views as *his* Defense Against the Dark Arts teaching position couldn't have helped his standing with the Potions Master.

Bellatrix asks why Snape didn't return at once when the Dark Lord was reborn. Of course, he *did* return, but he did so a couple of hours after the summons so that Dumbledore would think that he returned as a spy on Dumbledore's orders, thus ensuring that the headmaster continued to trust him, and giving Voldemort the continued advantage of a spy in his enemy's stronghold. Brilliantly, Snape also feigned a desire to prove to all present that the Dark Lord had returned (a revelation that, having already occurred, did not hurt the Death Eater cause) as an excuse to reveal his Dark Mark when it reappeared, and thus ensured that he would not have to hide it from anyone or be questioned about it.

The murder of Emmeline Vance, one of the few surviving members of the original Order of the Phoenix, is revealed as another one of Snape's sins. He was the one who notified the Death Eaters about her movements, which lead directly to her capture and death at the hands of his allies. This is the only murder that is specifically mentioned, but it's not a stretch to assume that his reports over time have led to other deaths as well.

Snape was not part of the battle to retrieve the prophecy for Voldemort inside the Ministry of Magic, and Bellatrix challenges him about his absence (she had been there, and killed Sirius Black). Snape states that his orders from Voldemort were to remain behind. These orders are certainly consistent with Voldemort's past orders that Snape stay out of the way of the action, and his participation would have alerted the Order to his true affiliation.

Why, Bellatrix asks, has Snape left Harry Potter alive? There are a few educated guesses detailed in a later section, but Snape specifically points out the simplest of them to Bellatrix: that murdering Harry would have exposed him and ended Dumbledore's trust in him, thus ending Snape's ability to gather information on Dumbledore, the Order of the Phoenix, and Harry Potter for his Dark Lord.

## Triple Agent for Voldemort

"But *he's* a very good Occlumens, isn't he, sir?" said Harry. . . .
"And isn't Voldemort convinced that Snape's on his side, even now? Professor . . . how can you be *sure* Snape's on our side?"

Dumbledore did not speak for a moment; he looked as though he was trying to make up his mind about something. At last he said, "I am sure. I trust Severus Snape completely."

—*Half-Blood Prince* (549)

Traditionally, a triple agent pretends to be a double agent for a target organization while working for a controlling organization all along, passing along just enough information to keep the trust of the target organization even as he or she works against them. In this case, Dumbledore believed that Snape was a double agent for the Order of the Phoenix, infiltrating the Death Eaters on his behalf. But Dumbledore, as stated before, is the trusting sort, while Voldemort is anything but trusting. Dumbledore is, by far, the easier to fool.

We know that Snape is hiding his true allegiance from either one or the other, Voldemort or Dumbledore. Based on their abilities, the likelihood is greater that he can and does hide it from Dumbledore. It would seem that Snape's outstanding abilities as both an Occlumens (someone capable of sealing the mind against magical intrusion and influence) and a Legilimens (a mind-reader) would guard him against all but the most skilled practitioners, indicating that he could utter falsehoods before Dumbledore, who would not normally stoop to being invasive, but not as easily before Voldemort, who would have no qualms about invading the thoughts of his followers. Voldemort would be far more difficult to cheat. Voldemort may be equal to Dumbledore in power, but while Dumbledore is a skilled Occlumens and Legilimens as well, Voldemort's exceptional abilities as the "'most accomplished Legilimens the world has ever seen'" (*Half-Blood Prince* 26) make him the harder wizard to fool.

Dumbledore states that Snape rejoined the side of good before Lord Voldemort's fall. What could cause such a change of heart? Severus had no cause to regret the death of James and Lily Potter. He openly despised James, and we witnessed him viciously insulting Lily when she spoke up in his defense in one of Snape's own memories. Any bond between Snape and the Potters could have only been of the negative sort. Why would there be such a shift of allegiance stemming from their deaths? Isn't it far more likely that Voldemort needed to place a man as near to Albus Dumbledore as possible, especially once the "one with the power to vanquish" him was eliminated, and so sent Snape there for that purpose? After all, Dumbledore had to be rather high on Voldemort's hit-list, and Snape made the perfect emissary.

Of course, Snape was always in a far better position to spy on Dumbledore than he ever was to spy on Voldemort. As a teacher he was at Hogwarts and near Dumbledore during most of the year, in the per-

fect place to keep tabs on his Dark Lord's enemy. On the other hand, he was not in regular communication with most Death Eaters and only reported in sporadically, and thus he would have been unable to gather much information on them. Snape also seems to have been the only spy Dumbledore had, while Voldemort had (and presumably still has) many. This suggests that—as might be expected of a Slytherin—Voldemort has far more skill in installing and cultivating spies than Dumbledore.

Snape certainly has much more of an incentive to serve the Dark Lord; if he does not satisfy Voldemort, he knows that he will be tortured and killed. Dumbledore, on the other hand, had little or no direct power over Snape or his behavior.

If Snape has been working for Dumbledore and the Order, he certainly hasn't done a very good job. Take a look at all the things Snape has failed to do over time. He didn't save James and Lily. He didn't tell Dumbledore about the Horcruxes, something he should have known about as a high-ranking Death Eater. He didn't teach Harry how to protect his mind during Occlumency lessons, leaving him undefended against Voldemort's trap at the Ministry. He didn't stop Harry from going to the Department of Mysteries. While Dumbledore believed him to truly be Voldemort's foe, Snape has never once actively thwarted any of Voldemort's plots. Snape demonstrates the exact behavior we'd expect from a skilled triple agent.

Snape wasn't the only Death Eater popularly believed to have turned on Voldemort after the Dark Lord's defeat. Igor Karkaroff, another former Death Eater who became headmaster of Durmstrang, even gave evidence against his fellow Death Eaters. But unlike Snape, Karkaroff was found dead soon after Voldemort returned to power. If Snape really is on Dumbledore's side, why is he still alive? Snape's role as an agent for Voldemort could not have been very widely known for the secret to be successfully kept, and one would think that a low-level Death Eater looking to gain favor with Voldemort would want to kill the traitor who had worked for Dumbledore for so long. That Voldemort has gone to the lengths needed to keep Snape protected indicates that Voldemort trusts Snape as far as he does anyone. After all, Voldemort is a difficult wizard to convince; he's the type to kill first, and ask questions later.

By *Half-Blood Prince*, Voldemort has assigned Wormtail to Snape as his assistant, and certainly Pettigrew could be there in part to spy on Snape. But Voldemort, as previously noted, is not a trusting man, and

Pettigrew's presence might be no more than a safeguard. Pettigrew himself has hardly been the most trustworthy minion. And ultimately, it's not entirely clear who is expected to watch who in that situation.

And thus we return to "Spinner's End" in *Half-Blood Prince*—aptly named as the chapter brings us to the end of the tale-spinner's story, the time when the truth is finally revealed. That truth, along with the events that transpired at its telling, led to Snape's worst crime yet: the murder of Dumbledore.

## Proof Positive: Killing Dumbledore

> But somebody else had spoken Snape's name, quite softly.
>
> "Severus . . ."
>
> The sound frightened Harry beyond anything he had experienced all evening. For the first time, Dumbledore was pleading.
>
> Snape said nothing, but walked forward and pushed Malfoy roughly out of the way. The three Death Eaters fell back without a word. Even the werewolf seemed cowed.
>
> Snape gazed for a moment at Dumbledore, and there was a revulsion and hatred etched in the harsh lines of his face.
>
> "Severus . . . please . . ."
>
> Snape raised his wand and pointed it directly at Dumbledore.
>
> "*Avada Kedavra!*"
>
> —*Half-Blood Prince* (595–596)

This horrible fact bears repeating; Snape killed Dumbledore. He murdered him using an Unforgivable Curse, with "revulsion and hatred" visibly apparent on his face. How can Snape be considered "good" after such an act? Good men do not commit murder. Not only that, but Dumbledore's death does far more harm than good in the fight against Voldemort. If Snape were indeed working on the side of good, the idea that Dumbledore's death was part of some grand plan defies logic.

Theories abound that Dumbledore chose to die for some higher purpose in some sort of Star Wars-esque homage to Obi-Wan Kenobi, yet another wise, white-bearded "wizard" ("If you strike me down," the old Jedi claimed, "I shall become more powerful than you could possibly imagine"). However, while it is a romantic notion, there are no practical reasons to support these "Dumbledore Chose to Die" theories.

Why would Dumbledore, the most powerful wizard in the world and the only wizard who is a match for Voldemort (Harry's status as "the Chosen One" notwithstanding), think it was a good idea to allow himself to be killed? Was it simply so Snape could better infiltrate the Death Eaters? The Order stood to gain too little and lose too much in this exchange. Dumbledore was of too much value to this fight, and he was never the type to shy away from the responsibility of leadership. And Dumbledore is the only wizard that Voldemort ever feared.

While the death of Dumbledore may rally the troops to fight on in his name, the Order of the Phoenix is now without their founder, Secret-Keeper, and leader. Plus, Dumbledore, as the wizard who brought Voldemort to Hogwarts and who taught him, knew their enemy better than anyone else, and was the only wizard who seems to have devised any kind of plan to fight him.

It also seems unlikely that Dumbledore summoned Snape to the tower in order to kill him. Although Dumbledore does indeed ask for Snape several times upon his final return to Hogwarts, he has just ingested a poisonous potion during his attempt to retrieve one of Voldemort's Horcruxes. Who better to ask for than Snape, his supposedly loyal former Potions Master who, due to his past involvement with the Death Eaters, would have the best chance of brewing a viable antidote?

Dumbledore has left many loose threads behind. The remaining Horcruxes still need to be found, and Harry is ill-equipped to find them without Dumbledore's aid. It would be foolish for Dumbledore to plot his own death without leaving all the information necessary to win the fight for those left behind.

It could be argued that his lessons with Harry that year are just that, but Harry has far too many unanswered questions and far too little truly useful knowledge for that to be a viable point. Either that or, if the lessons *were* supposed to prepare Harry for Dumbledore's absence, Dumbledore failed miserably in his intent.

Dumbledore's death increased the level of fear in the wizarding community, which already acts far too cowed to mount any kind of resistance to Voldemort. The common wizard is terrified: anyone could be cursed at any moment, the fear-inducing Dark Mark might appear anywhere, Dementors are loose, and under the influence of Dark magic, children are killing their own parents. Then, the most powerful wizard not named Voldemort is murdered not only at his

own fortress, but at what is supposedly the "safest" place in the wizarding world, by a long-time Hogwarts teacher. What could be more demoralizing to those left behind?

If you examine the events as they unfolded that terrible day, they do not reveal a Snape who in any way worked for the side of good. When he learns of what is happening on the tower, Snape rushes to fulfill his vow, stupefying Professor Flitwick and tricking Luna and Hermione in order to join the fight more quickly. While it might have been easier to kill them at that point, such early action would have revealed his true allegiance and, had Dumbledore *not* been killed, Snape would not have been able to stay at Hogwarts as a spy.

When Snape kills Dumbledore, it's important to note that he doesn't use an easy or uncertain method. He uses *Avada Kedavra*, one of the series's three "Unforgivable Curses." These curses are among the most powerful Dark spells that exist and are so named because their use is completely unforgivable in the wizarding world. Use of any of these spells on a sentient being carries an automatic life sentence in Azkaban. Due to their power, their use requires strong desire, directed will, and enormous skill.

So how could a "good" Snape summon up the hatred necessary to use such a horrible curse to kill the headmaster? We see Harry attempt to use an Unforgivable Curse on Bellatrix during the fight at the Ministry, but he is incapable of pulling it off; as angry as Harry is, as much as he hates Bellatrix, he cannot summon enough anger and hatred to successfully cast the spell. If Snape is good, it seems unlikely that he would have summoned the necessary feelings to successfully curse a man he loved and respected.

Also, why bother to use such a powerful curse, with Dumbledore already sorely weakened by poison? Even if Snape had to kill Dumbledore, even if Dumbledore had asked it of him, surely there were less Unforgivable, even less final, ways to do so. Instead, Snape kills him by guaranteed means, so that there could be no doubt; according to Rowling, Dumbledore is indeed dead (and he will not, as Rowling herself put it during her 2006 appearance at Radio City Music Hall, "pull a Gandalf").

Remember, the revulsion in Snape's face focuses on Dumbledore. To Snape, the headmaster represents all that was unfair in his life, from the torment he endured as a youth right under the man's nose to being

repeatedly denied the Defense Against the Dark Arts position he'd wanted for so long in favor of insultingly less-qualified replacements. After years of kowtowing to Dumbledore because he had no choice, first to convince Dumbledore to take him in and then to maintain the façade of a working relationship for years, Snape could finally let his true feelings show. With such strong emotions fueling it, the Unforgivable Curse worked like a charm.

What does Dumbledore mean by his final words, "'Severus . . . please . . .'"? It's far more than simply a plea for mercy. After all, Dumbledore took Snape in and trusted him when no one else did, giving him a respected place at Hogwarts and a vital position in the Order of the Phoenix. Faced with Snape's betrayal, Dumbledore would, being Dumbledore, plead with Snape to reconsider or, if he knew about the Unbreakable Vow, find a way around it—believing in Snape's better nature to the last. But Snape does not reconsider, and he does not hesitate.

But what about that pesky Unbreakable Vow? If Snape is on Dumbledore's side, and knows in advance about Draco's task (as he claims early in the "Spinner's End" conversation), why would he take the vow at all? With his skill at manipulating conversation, he could have avoided it. With his skills as a Legilimens, he could have steered the conversation away from it completely. He *chose* not to avoid it.

During his conversation with Narcissa and Bellatrix at Spinner's End, Snape has many chances to put Narcissa off. If Snape was on Dumbledore's side, he could have simply told Narcissa that the Dark Lord gave the mission to Draco, and therefore Snape could not disobey the Dark Lord by assuming the task himself. But instead, he answers, "'He intends me to do it in the end, I think'" (34). Snape could just as easily have repeated what Bellatrix told Narcissa, that Draco must be the one to complete the task and that it is an honor to be asked to do work for the Dark Lord. Either of these statements would have provided a perfectly believable cover for his loyalty to Dumbledore without committing to taking any action himself. But he says instead: "'It might be possible . . . for me to help Draco'" (35). He *volunteers*. Snape would have known full well, saying this, what the consequences would be. And when Narcissa mentions the Unbreakable Vow, Snape willingly accepts.

He has a variety of possible reasons to agree to take the Vow. First, because helping to kill Dumbledore would be a pleasure for any true follower of the Dark Lord. Second, because it would avenge Snape for years

of subjugation at Dumbledore's hands while Snape's talents lay unused. And third, perhaps most importantly, because by completing the plan to kill Dumbledore if Draco faltered, Snape would not only fulfill the Vow, but also seize the victorious moment for himself. Dumbledore would have been a dead man whether Snape killed him or not. Remember, Draco and several other Death Eaters show up to confront Dumbledore before Snape ever arrives. Any one of them could and would have killed him if Snape hadn't stepped up to the plate and done it first. Instead of bickering like the other Death Eaters, Snape assesses the situation and seizes the glory for himself in the way Draco had feared he would all year long (why else would Draco refuse his help with such a difficult task?).

Snape can now be heralded as the killer of the leader of the enemy force. Whatever mild irritation Vodlemort might feel at Lucius Malfoy's punishment having been derailed would mean little in the face of his greatest enemy's death. Think of the coup this was, both for Snape and for the Death Eaters as a whole. Think of how much higher Snape can now rise in the organization. Dumbledore is the only wizard who was ever able to stand up to Voldemort at the height of his power. Snape removed Voldemort's biggest obstacle.

Interestingly, McGonagall, Lupin, Hagrid, and Tonks all easily accept Snape's guilt after Dumbledore's death. They express varying degrees of shock, certainly, but none of them display much in the way of disbelief at the news. After all, their previous belief in Snape's trustworthiness was predicated on Dumbledore's inexplicable faith in him to begin with. Without Dumbledore present to insist otherwise, what these witches and wizards know of Snape from their own experience allows them to see this sudden treachery as a perfectly plausible turn of events.

### Hating Harry

Snape hates Harry Potter. He is cruel to Harry as a professor, taunting him unmercifully, and is always contemptuous of his work. He gives Harry and his friends frequent and often unjustified detentions and, on several occasions, has tried to have Harry expelled from Hogwarts. Why did Harry become his target?

Snape started his habit of hating Potters early. James Potter and Snape hated each other immediately when they met at Hogwarts, at least

according to Sirius Black, and Snape's inability to forgive James for bullying and embarrassing him in school (even after having caused his death), and his transference of his hatred onto James's son, is one of the most negative aspects of Snape's nature. "'How extraordinarily like your father you are, Potter,' Snape said suddenly, his eyes glinting. 'He too was exceedingly arrogant. A small amount of talent on the Quidditch field made him think he was a cut above the rest of us too. Strutting around the place with his friends and admirers. . . . The resemblance between you is uncanny'" (*Prisoner of Azkaban* 284).

Worst of all (to Snape), Harry's father once saved Snape's life in the middle of a particularly dangerous prank, stopping Snape before he could be torn apart by a werewolf, although James was also in on the joke at first. "'When one wizard saves another wizard's life, it creates a certain bond between them,'" Dumbledore explains in *Prisoner of Azkaban* (427). Owing a life debt to his worst enemy must have infuriated Snape all the more.

His wish for vengeance on James extended to his entire schoolyard gang, including Sirius Black and Remus Lupin, and drove Snape to irrationality even in adulthood. During confrontations with his former school foes in several books, Snape has a mad glint in his eyes, losing all appearance of reason, and this hatred regularly affects his actions. In *Prisoner of Azkaban*, he assigns an essay on werewolves while substituting for Lupin, hoping Lupin's students will catch on to the reason for Lupin's regular absences (only Hermione does), and works to have Sirius Black captured, nearly summoning Dementors to have his soul removed. Lupin asks him, "'Is a schoolboy grudge worth putting an innocent man back inside Azkaban?'" (359). Snape's answer, apparently, is yes.

Snape, sadly, has never stopped acting like a vindictive little boy who will do whatever it takes to gain respect, behaving the bully in front of the classroom just as he was bullied all those years ago. And Snape's unconscious actions express his hatred as much as his conscious ones do, especially the constant expression of utter loathing on his face when he looks at Harry.

Interestingly, some readers believe that Snape was in love with Lily Evans Potter from their time together at Hogwarts and that Snape's treatment of Harry stems from a grudge about her marrying his rival. While this is a lovely thought, Snape's actions do not support it.

Were Snape actually in love with Lily, wouldn't he treat her only son, a child who has his mother's eyes, better than he does? He treats Harry poorly from the moment they meet. Wouldn't he avoid pointlessly harassing Lily's only son, even if it is just for her sake? According to Horace Slughorn, Lily was extremely talented at brewing potions and one of the brightest students the old professor had ever taught. Why wouldn't Snape encourage that sort of ability in her son instead of berating him for every mistake?

Not to mention, it's very unlikely for Snape to have fallen in love with Lily in the first place. Lily was a "Mudblood," born to Muggle parents. How could Snape, a true Slytherin (albeit a half-blood one) who threw his lot in with the zealously purity-minded Lord Voldemort, love someone with full Muggle lineage?

However, putting all thoughts of past grudges and possible loves aside, Snape's most critical reason for hating Harry is the possibility that Harry, as the "Chosen One" named in Trelawney's prophecy, may ultimately defeat Voldemort. Voldemort is Snape's "Dark Lord"; Snape has given him his loyalty, and, as double (or triple) agent, has sacrificed any semblance of a normal life in order to do Voldemort's work.

Snape's father abused him emotionally and likely physically as well. His teachers at Hogwarts rewarded the students who tormented him while brushing him aside as unimportant. Voldemort was the first authority figure to accept Snape for who he was and welcome him, giving him a position of responsibility and a place in the world. Snape would despise the mere idea of his Dark Lord's defeat and thus hate Harry as the boy who could cause it.

### Then Why Protect Harry? Repeatedly?

Undeniably, Snape has often taken action to protect Harry during his first years at Hogwarts, despite his obvious hatred of the boy. Why not just allow Harry to die? Snape has had plenty of opportunities to do just that. But, as much as Snape might enjoy killing the son of his rival, Snape knows about the prophecy concerning Voldemort and Harry, and he knows that killing Harry is not his task to fulfill.

Of course, killing Harry would have destroyed Dumbledore's trust and blown his cover, but the reasons go much deeper than that. First of all, Voldemort needed Harry in order to fully return to life and power;

he uses him for just that purpose after the Triwizard Tournament. Had Harry died before then, Voldemort might have found another way, but not necessarily one that would have allowed him to return so immediately and with such power. Snape needed to keep Harry safe until the time was right.

According to Snape, Voldemort had expressly forbidden his followers from killing Harry Potter. "'Have you forgotten our orders? Potter belongs to the Dark Lord—we are to leave him!'" (*Half-Blood Prince* 603). After all, as Trelawney's prophecy states, "'EITHER MUST DIE AT THE HAND OF THE OTHER FOR NEITHER CAN LIVE WHILE THE OTHER SURVIVES'" (*Order of the Phoenix* 841).

One fascinating theory is that Harry himself is a Horcrux for Voldemort, making his safety of paramount importance to anyone who knows the secret and is loyal to Voldemort. The creation of a Horcrux occurs when one rips the soul by committing an intensely evil act, such as murder, and then encases a piece of that soul in an object. The object can be anything, animate or inanimate; Voldemort, megalomaniac that he is, chose only those objects he thought to be worthy of the honor. Dumbledore tells Harry that Voldemort was still at least one Horcrux short of his goal when he entered the Potter home with the intention of killing Harry. The power necessary to make baby Harry into a Horcrux could have been generated by the murder of his mother. Also, as Lord Voldemort prefers to make Horcruxes out of either items tied to Hogwarts or trophies that commemorate significant murders, and Harry is a vital part of the prophecy that foretold his defeat, the body of the Chosen One may be the most meaningful object of all. It is implied that Voldemort became less human with each Horcrux he created; Harry could have been the final Horcrux, one strong and vital enough that Voldemort all but ceased to be.

This theory would explain a great deal about Harry's bond with Voldemort, as well as why Harry's scar itches and burns when Voldemort is active or feeling intense emotions. In fact, the scar could be directly tied to the creation of the Horcrux; we have heard of no other scars when the Killing Curse has been used, as we are told (and have witnessed) that its victims simply drop dead.

Harry's greatest strength at Hogwarts is Defense Against the Dark Arts, a subject in which he eclipses even Hermione and which he has taught to other students at their request. How better to excel at Defense

Against the Dark Arts than to innately understand what it is that you defend against?

If part of Voldemort resides in Harry, it would also explain how Harry has been able to see through the eyes of Nagini, the serpent believed to serve as Voldemort's familiar and possibly also as one of Voldemort's Horcruxes. It would also explain how Harry became a Parselmouth, an exceedingly rare talent and one that he shares with Voldemort; in fact, as far as we have been told, the only Parselmouths currently living are Voldemort and Harry.

This theory has a great deal to support it, considering the number of ties between the two wizards. Voldemort and Harry possess wands that are "brothers"—they each contain a tail feather from the phoenix Fawkes. Also, the Sorting Hat considers placing Harry in Slytherin, even though both of his parents were in Gryffindor: "'Not Slytherin, eh? . . . Are you sure? You could be great, you know, it's all here in your head'" (*Sorcerer's Stone* 121). You have to wonder what it is that the Sorting Hat sees in Harry's head. Perhaps a part of Voldemort himself?

Remember, too, this scene in Dumbledore's office in *Order of the Phoenix*:

> At once, Harry's scar burned white-hot, as though the old wound had burst open again—and unbidden, unwanted, but terrifyingly strong, there rose within Harry a hatred so powerful he felt, for that instant, that he would like nothing better than to strike—to bite— to sink his fangs in the man before him [Dumbledore] (474-475).

As Harry explains to Sirius later, "'It was like something rose up inside me, like there's a *snake* inside me—'" (481).

Voldemort also possesses Harry at the end of the battle at the Department of Mysteries without any apparent spell. He accomplished this remotely, without having any direct physical control over Harry at the time. Although Voldemort is extremely powerful, we have no evidence that he is able to possess people at will from a distance. The only other times we have seen him use a similar power are in the case of Professor Quirrell, whose body he takes over physically as well as mentally, and in the case of Ginny Weasley, who he possesses using the tangible connection of his diary. If he has no such limits on his power, why wouldn't he simply possess people whenever it suits his needs? One logical explanation for how Voldemort was able to possess Harry in such an

unprecedented fashion is the ability to link his consciousness with the fragment of his own soul already inside Harry.

Even though Voldemort has tried to kill Harry since the night of his mother's death—including during the battle at the Ministry of Magic when he tries the *Avada Kedavra*—Harry's corpse (or his scar alone) might still work as a Horcrux and remain a safe vessel for a segment of Voldemort's soul. After all, a Horcrux is nothing more than a container.

Dumbledore believed that Voldemort used something from each of the four Houses of Hogwarts, and indeed, to continue Rowling's ongoing theme of the Houses working together, this should be the case. However, the only objects that Godric Gryffindor left behind were the Sorting Hat and his sword, both of which remain safely stored in Dumbledore's office. Voldemort may have substituted the son of two Gryffindors for his final House-related Horcrux.

If Harry is indeed a Horcrux for Voldemort, that fact alone would give Snape every reason to watch over Harry carefully . . . if he knows this secret, of course. Considering that he has been called "Voldemort's most trusted advisor," by a fellow Death Eater, he is likely one of the few—or even the only one—in on this critical secret. Snape may also think that Harry is not worthy of such an honor, much as he felt that Quirrell was unworthy of the Sorcerer's Stone, giving us yet another reason for the dreadful way Snape treats Harry throughout the years. And, if Harry is a Horcrux, Voldemort would have stronger cause to need his blood in order to become fully corporeal and functional again, and this could be the reason behind his strict orders that none of his loyal followers kill this often-vulnerable threat to their Dark Lord. The piece of soul in Harry's head would give Snape every reason to keep Harry alive. Of course, it would still be perfectly acceptable to keep him miserable, something Snape delights in doing.

### An Auxiliary Theory: The Free Agent

Snape, while certainly a villain, might not be entirely focused on Voldemort's aims. As he embodies Slytherin's ambitious attitude, it is possible that Snape is not fully working for Voldemort but rather just taking the opportunity the situation presents to better his own position. This motivation, however, does not change any of the basic facts. Snape is an evil man.

Working for Voldemort brought him power and prestige as a high-

ranking Death Eater, and working for Dumbledore, however distasteful, saved him from Azkaban and gave him a comfortable position in the wizarding world at large. While his nature swings him closer to Voldemort's side, he could be playing both, using the side that brings him the most advantage and benefits without caring who the ultimate victor might be. As such, his secret neutrality serves no good except his own, and as John F. Kennedy noted in 1963 in Bonn, West Germany, "Dante once said that the hottest places in hell are reserved for those who in a period of moral crisis maintain their neutrality."

# Part II: The Literary Argument

It's fun to write about Snape because he's a deeply horrible person.
—J. K. ROWLING, *Family Education*, 1999

Has Rowling already given us the answer to the great Snape question? At the very least, she has given us quite a few very large clues. But while plenty of evidence exists within the books themselves that could convict Snape in a trial, clues that lead to his true nature extend well beyond the circumstances and motivations presented in the plot. The structure of the books, the character compositions, and the methods of plot and character revelation point to Snape's villainy as well.

## Why "Good Snape" Is Far Less Interesting Than "Evil Snape"

Rowling delights in confounding readers, revealing aspects of characters that we would have never suspected and surprising us at every turn: the identity of Tom Riddle, Sirius Black being good, Peter Pettigrew being both alive and evil (and Scabbers), the false Mad-Eye Moody, Lupin the Werewolf, the shocking lack of belief by the wizarding population that Voldemort has returned after the Triwizard Tournament, etc. Throughout the series, she liberally uses misdirection and challenges our expectations. Most of all, she has used this strategy with Snape.

In the first book of the Harry Potter series, a large part of the plot revolved around one question: "Is Snape evil?" Of course, the answer in the first book appears to be no. Based on all of the obvious clues—appearance, manner, and his instant and seemingly inexplicable hatred of our hero—we are fooled into believing that Snape is the villain. The

true villain in this instance, of course, turns out to be the previously unsuspected Professor Quirrell and the piece of Lord Voldemort hiding inside him.

Snape possesses a particular loathing for Harry, making us automatically doubt his motivations, but, after saving our hero during the Quidditch match and the unmasking of the true villain, we are meant to think that Snape is in actuality simply a grouchy good guy with a chip on his shoulder. As the books progress, questions continue to rise, but each is discounted or explained away by Dumbledore.

Snape has been falsely accused repeatedly. After so many instances of his name being cleared, are we really supposed to believe that Rowling will use the same pattern again as events come to a head? The most effective twist, considering the ones that have come before it, would be the revelation that Snape is evil despite all the times he has previously been cleared of wrongdoing, not the revelation that he is good, as has been insisted upon by Dumbledore.

The answer about Snape's innocence or guilt should not be the same after the final book as it was after the first book. Snape's "apparent" evilness can only mislead readers so many times. We are not meant to be deceived by Snape's villainous appearance, which is so obvious that we can't help but question it, but rather, we are meant to be deceived by the *impression* of villainy. After all, how can someone who looks so perfectly evil actually *be* evil?

As the sixth book begins, this question remains despite the multiple times that Snape has protected Harry and despite Dumbledore's repeated declarations of faith. Our opinion of him has softened, now that we know that Snape had an unhappy childhood, and that he was bullied while a student at Hogwarts—by Harry's father, no less. We are in a better position to understand Snape's hatred of Harry, who reminds him of his schoolyard nemesis, and Snape seems simply petty and vindictive and sad, not evil.

But in the closing moments of *Half-Blood Prince*, we discover a new Snape, and *this* Snape is a real surprise. His clear statements in "Spinner's End" may have misdirected some readers to discount them as lies, especially as we were without Harry, our official guide in this world, during the scene, but instead, the truth of the statements becomes clear. With Dumbledore's murder, we see the scope of Snape's true intentions and, after so many exonerating circumstances and lesser villains scattered

about to mislead us throughout the series, Snape reveals his true colors at long last, and they turn out to be as dark as his robes.

Snape *seems* the perfect anti-hero, the perfect complex character, following the redemptive path that seems so popular in fiction these days, found everywhere from Darth Vader in Star Wars to Spike in *Buffy the Vampire Slayer*. This is a comfortable pattern for us to follow because we have become accustomed to it, but Rowling rarely lets us remain comfortable. Snape is not yet another anti-hero of modern fiction; instead, he is far more interesting: an expertly cloaked villain like *Batman Begins*'s Ra's al Ghul, or Star Wars's Senator Palpatine. After being abused at home, tormented in school, and frustrated as a young adult, he chose a path that would give him the power he did not possess as a child, a path any Slytherin would understand. He chose to side with Voldemort, and he did so in a way that gave him advantages on both sides.

## The Need for a Great Villain

> You have a choice when you're going to introduce a very evil character. You can dress a guy up with loads of ammunition, put a black Stetson on him, and say, "Bad guy. Shoot him." I'm writing about shades of evil. You have Voldemort, a raging psychopath, devoid of the normal human responses to other people's suffering, and there are people like that in the world. But then you have Wormtail, who out of cowardice will stand in the shadow of the strongest person.
> —J. K. ROWLING, *Entertainment Weekly*, 2000

Every great story needs a great villain. The Harry Potter books have told an undeniably great story so far, but Lord Voldemort is, quite frankly, a weak villain. This is not a reflection of the character's power in the world of the story but rather the character's power *as* a character. While we know his actions and history, we do not know *him*.

Readers are not the least bit invested in Voldemort. While we had a brief chance to get to know the boy he once was, Tom Riddle, the Dark wizard he became as an adult does not resemble him in looks or even in name, severing any connection to him we may have tenuously built. He's a stereotypical villain, a larger-than-life figure that menaces from afar. Much like Sauron in Lord of the Rings (primarily seen in the recent films as nothing more than a big red eyeball), he possesses near-omnipotence

and seeks to utterly dominate his realm not by personal involvement, but by means of his devoted followers.

But readers *are* invested in Snape. After six books of Snape's constant presence as a thorn in Harry's side, after six books of being consistently defended and acquitted by Harry's mentor, Snape's emergence as a villain would make the final installment of the saga far more interesting than if Voldemort remained the only primary villain.

Snape makes a superb archenemy for Harry. To continue the Lord of the Rings comparison, he serves the same function as Saruman, pretending to work on the side of good until he shows his true colors by acting in opposition to the powers of good. Snape can also be compared to Long John Silver of *Treasure Island*, who earns the trust of Captain John Flint and bonds with young Jim Hawkins (Snape, of course, skipped the "bonding" part) but leads the mutiny against Flint and kills him, forcing Jim to confront and fight him later on.

A good villain should have strong feelings toward the hero one way or another, but while Voldemort sees Harry as troublesome and a possible danger, there are no real emotions there. When Voldemort tries to kill Harry at the Ministry, he says, "'You have irked me too often, for too long'" just before attempting the Killing Curse on him (*Order of the Phoenix* 813). "Irked" is not exactly the word a sworn enemy would use. Conversely, Snape clearly and unapologetically despises Harry, and that hatred is returned. Their conflict is loaded with emotion on both sides, as Snape and Harry have a long history of personal conflict to draw from. In addition, Snape also has his bitter childhood conflict with Harry's father that fuels his hatred of Harry further.

Imagine if Voldemort and Snape both lost their ability to practice magic. Would Voldemort still interest us? We have no real tie to him; if he can't properly threaten the lives of Harry and the other characters we've grown to love, there's no reason to care about him at all. But even without his magic, Snape would still fascinate us. We need to see at least two sides to every person, and Voldemort possesses only one: extreme, pure evil. Voldemort remains more of a caricature than a fully fleshed-out character.

Snape is far more complicated and thus far more interesting. He is human rather than superhuman. Voldemort has acted chiefly as a plot device, driving the circumstances of each book at a remove, primarily through others, while Snape has been Harry's constant personal nemesis

throughout the series. A great villain should not be evil without reason or simply by nature. Voldemort is evil, pure and simple, and he has never shown himself to be otherwise, even as a child. Snape clearly became who and what he is as a result of his upbringing, school ties, and personal choices.

Even the structure of the characters' names makes Snape the opposite to Harry, as their most frequently used names have the same number of letters (H-A-R-R-Y and S-N-A-P-E). Voldemort is Dumbledore's enemy: their names are tied together linguistically, each possessing three syllables and a similar vowel pattern (and if you pronounce "Voldemort" the way Rowling originally intended, dropping the "t," they even rhyme!). By the same token, Harry's true nemesis must be Snape.

Most importantly, a great villain should be a memorable character (a really great villain is sometimes more memorable than the story's hero), and no character captivates us more than Severus Snape. He sweeps into each scene carrying his secret with him, wearing his villainy as clearly as his standard villain attire while somehow hiding behind them both, making his intentions and allegiance the pivotal question as we wait for *Deathly Hallows*.

Snape is one of the most memorable characters, if not *the* most memorable, in the entire Harry Potter series; as Rowling herself says, Snape is "a gift of a character" (Edinburgh Book Festival, 2004). Only a villain such as this could make the series complete; as a hero, reluctant or not, the series would ultimately lack balance.

Snape's villainy has been hidden in the cleverest place possible: in plain sight. The clues have all been present for us to read, but it has been far easier for us to focus on the obvious and extreme villainy of Voldemort. With the trusting Dumbledore's stamp of approval in place, Snape was able to hide his villainy from everyone, including readers, until it was too late.

We want to believe in character redemption, but redemption requires not only great strength, but also great selflessness. Some characters just don't have it in them to follow such a path. We want to believe in Dumbledore, the powerful mentor figure, just as we want to believe in our own mentors and parental figures, but part of growing up is learning that our mentors are not infallible. We don't like to believe that our hero has been in danger from the beginning, in the place he has loved

most and by someone we were told to trust, but we know that danger has always surrounded Harry. We just didn't realize how close that danger was.

Snape has certainly protected Harry, but he has done so for his own reasons and each of them has either directly or indirectly served the Dark Lord's plans. Harry has value. But Snape has killed the leader of Voldemort's opposition, Dumbledore, scoring a great victory for the Death Eaters by disposing of their greatest enemy.

While Voldemort has made grand evil gestures, manipulated events from the background, and threatened from afar, moving his followers around like chess pieces, Snape has always been Harry's true antagonist. Snape and Harry have been in a battle of wills from the very beginning, and their battle has evolved and deepened while Harry's opposition to Voldemort has not varied. If Voldemort is defeated, we will cheer, certainly, but how much will we care? In order for us to have a completely satisfactory conclusion to the series, it must be Severus Snape that Harry faces at the very end. Snape must be the foe that Harry defeats.

## Top Ten Reasons Why We Love to Hate Snape

1. "Snape gazed for a moment at Dumbledore, and there was revulsion and hatred etched in the harsh lines of his face. . . . Snape raised his wand and pointed it directly at Dumbledore. 'Avada Kedavra!'" (*Half-Blood Prince* 595–596). Oh, snap! Oh, Snape! The most famous betrayal since Judas.

2. Throws Harry against the wall when he catches him snooping into his memory of being humiliated by James Potter in *Order of the Phoenix*. Let this be a lesson to us all: Remember to put on clean underpants *every day*.

3. Reduces Neville Longbottom to the verge of tears when he threatens to feed his botched Shrinking Solution to his pet toad in *Prisoner of Azkaban*. Neville retaliates by imagining his Boggart Snape wearing ladies' clothes. Which is better than being hung upside down with your dirty underpants showing, but only marginally.

4. Gives Harry detention every Saturday when Harry refuses to turn over his copy of *Advanced Potion-Making*, causing him to miss the last Quidditch match of the year. "Poor Gryffindor . . . fourth place this year, I fear . . .'" (*Half-Blood Prince* 528). Stay tuned for the shocking revelations in Book Seven: not only was Snape illegally betting on Slytherin, he juiced their brooms and had Draco on steroids.

5. Tries to have Harry and Ron expelled from Hogwarts after they crash the Flying Ford Anglia into the Whomping Willow in *Chamber of Secrets*. Ah, Snape's just jealous. He's been itching to drive a car ever since he saw *Herbie: Fully Loaded*.

## Top Ten Reasons Why We Love to Hate Snape (Con't.)

6. Accuses Professor Lupin of helping Sirius Black enter Hogwarts and threatens to turn them both over to the authorities in *Prisoner of Azkaban*. "'You fool,' said Lupin softly. 'Is a schoolboy grudge worth putting an innocent man back inside Azkaban?'" (359). Well, yes, as a matter of fact it is. Any other questions, Wolfboy?

7. Confiscates Hermione's copy of *Witch Weekly* and reads Rita Skeeter's latest column about Harry aloud to the class, eliciting gales of laughter from the Slytherins in *Goblet of Fire*. They were probably just relieved that Snape wasn't reading them his unpublished novel again.

8. Lets it "slip" that Lupin is a werewolf, forcing him to resign from the staff of Hogwarts in *Prisoner of Azkaban*. Lesser-known fact: Madame Hooch was fired after Snape spread a rumor that she was really a Hobbit, explaining why she hasn't been seen since the first movie.

9. Gives the Dark Lord the prophecy he overheard from Sybill Trelawney, causing Voldemort to go after James and Lily Potter's baby son. Oddly enough, Snape didn't think the rest of the prophecy—"If you harm Harry Potter, you will be reduced to a bodyless head"—was worth repeating.

10. "'I see no difference.'" Snape's reaction to Hermione's beaver teeth, after she's caught in the crossfire of Harry and Draco's spells in *Goblet of Fire* (300). *America's Next Top Model*, meet your newest judge.

# II.
# SNAPE THE VILLAIN

LIKE SCARS AND BAD MEMORIES, the Dark Mark is forever.

Professor Dumbledore trusts Severus Snape. But Harry Potter doesn't for a moment buy Snape's alleged conversion from follower of Lord Voldemort to spy for Dumbledore. It doesn't matter to Harry that Snape keeps saving his neck. Snape sold out Harry's parents to Voldemort. And he bullies and torments Harry with impunity, viciously insulting the memory of James Potter whenever he can. Besides, reasons Harry, isn't Snape head of Slytherin House, from which Voldemort has always drawn his followers? Indeed, in *Goblet of Fire*, Snape rolls up his sleeve to reveal the skull and snake of the Dark Mark, burned into his flesh when he became one of the Dark Lord's Death Eaters. Maybe Snape fooled Dumbledore with his confession of remorse over providing Voldemort with the information that led to James and Lily Potter's death. But, as far as Harry is concerned, Snape's true loyalty isn't just written on his forearm, it's written on his soul.

J. K. Rowling's descriptions of Snape do little to contradict Harry's perception of the Potions Master as a classically sinister villain. In our first glimpse of Snape in *Sorcerer's Stone*, we see that he is "hook-nosed" and "sallow" with "greasy black hair" (126); later in the book, Rowling describes Snape's eyes as "cold and empty" and resembling "dark tunnels" (136). He speaks in "barely more than a whisper" (136), unless he's angry, in which case he shrieks, roars, and looks "quite deranged" (*Prisoner of Azkaban* 360). He is "[c]ruel, sarcastic, and disliked by everybody except for students from his own house" (*Chamber of Secrets* 77). When he passes by, it's as if his black robes are "rippling in a cold breeze" (*Chamber of Secrets* 78). He glides, hisses, snarls, slithers, storms, spits, and sneers. He is compared to a bat, a snake, and a spider.

Throughout the first four books of the saga, Rowling uses language like this to strip Snape of his humanity. And then, in *Order of the Phoenix*, she gives it back to him. She shows us Snape's worst memory in excruciating detail, and it's a surprisingly typical, but intensely painful, teenage-bullying episode to which we can all relate. Sneaking a look into the Pensieve, Harry sees Snape as a fifteen-year-old misfit, a weird kid with "lank and greasy" hair and a "stringy, pallid look about him" (640) who arrived at Hogwarts knowing more about the Dark Arts than anybody else. As Harry watches with increasing discomfort, we see "Snivellus" being teased and tormented by the swaggering James Potter in front of a crowd of schoolmates, including Lily

Evans, the popular girl on whom every boy seems to have a crush. Snape tries to fight back against James's spells, but his adversary gets the better of him; James hangs Snape upside down with a *Levicorpus* spell and Snape's robes fall open to reveal "skinny, pallid legs" and "graying underpants" (647). Everyone (except Lily) laughs. "Snape was clearly unpopular," Rowling tells us (646). "'Who wants to see me take off Snivelly's [under]pants?'" James is crowing as the scene comes to an abrupt close (649).

The adult Snape can't put this humiliation behind him. His hatred of James is as fresh as it was when he was fifteen. In a display of bitterness and stunted emotional growth, Snape takes his revenge on James by picking on Harry. In *Order of the Phoenix*, Rowling also has Harry penetrate Snape's mind during an Occlumency lesson, glimpsing memories of the Potions Master as a young child who cries as his father threatens his cowering mother, and as a lonely youth who sits in a darkened bedroom, killing bugs with his wand. Rowling is showing us the emotional wounds that have festered inside Snape all these years; it's the sort of pain that makes people feel powerless and without hope, makes them easy prey for recruitment by tyrants (terrorists?) like Voldemort. Rowling is also suggesting that bullying breeds bullying, using the sad example of Snape punishing Harry to avenge his own ordeal at the hands of James. We are meant to feel a twinge of sympathy, as Harry does, for Snape; it's tempting to view him as a victim. But, at the same time, Rowling makes it clear that Harry has had a pretty rotten childhood himself, yet still manages to rise above misery and self-pity; so far, Harry hasn't tried to dull his pain by being cruel to others. So, Rowling asks, is Snape really deserving of our sympathy?

Nothing about Snape is clear-cut, including our feelings about him; he's like a tangle of string that becomes more knotted the more we try to unravel it. By keeping his true loyalties in doubt (Harry's suspicion is balanced by Dumbledore's trust, and vice versa), Rowling has made Snape the perfect enigma. She has made sure that he is a blank screen, upon which we can project the motives and loyalties we wish to see. That's why some readers were able to watch Snape killing Dumbledore and still look for an explanation to exonerate him. As frustrating as it is trying to figure out what Snape is really all about, it's also a heck of a lot of fun. Snape is far more complex than the obvious villain he appears to be on first glance. If he weren't so complex, readers would have closed

*Half-Blood Prince* unanimously able to accept his guilt. And the Harry Potter saga would have been a lot less interesting.

## The Fallen

Rowling has slyly created Snape as a two-headed coin. Both of the faces Snape presents to the world—remorse-filled good guy, unrepentant bad guy—seem valid. And that's not just because he's a double agent and a "'superb Occlumens'" (*Order of the Phoenix* 527) who knows how to keep his true nature locked up beneath layers of contradictions and lies. It's because both possible interpretations of Snape, hero and villain, spring from the same literary traditions. The tradition that lets us consider Snape as a possible anti-hero can be traced back to John Milton's partly sympathetic portrayal of Satan in his epic poem *Paradise Lost* (1667). But Snape's manner of villain can be traced back to Milton's Satan as well.

In the first three sections of *Paradise Lost*, Satan captivates us with his charisma, courage, intellect, and ambition as he struggles against the tyranny of God. But Satan overreaches in his quest to corrupt humankind, and our sympathies fall away as we see him for the villain— the serpent—that he is. His towering pride, envy, and appetite for vengeance are his downfall. Like Milton's Satan, Snape is fiercely intelligent, proud, and ambitious. (And let's not forget that the Slytherin symbol is a snake.) In *Sorcerer's Stone*, Snape tells his Potions students that he can teach them how to "'bottle fame, brew glory, even stopper death'" (137), and as the series goes on and we learn more about him, we realize that in this speech Snape has revealed his own ambition for immortal fame and glory in that boast. Like Satan, Snape is also a persuasive and articulate speaker. In the "Spinner's End" chapter of *Half-Blood Prince*, Rowling lets Snape speak for himself, and lets us evaluate him through our own eyes rather than Harry's biased ones. And Snape gives an awe-inspiring performance of bravado and nerve.

In "Spinner's End," Snape faces Death Eater Bellatrix Lestrange's suspicions about his true loyalties. Snape smoothly offers Bellatrix explanations and justifications for every questionable action, from his failure to join the Death Eaters at the graveyard when Voldemort was resurrected, to his repeated protection of Harry, to a coziness with Dumbledore that seems to go above and beyond his duties as Voldemort's spy. Snape

answers all these accusations without flinching and he seals his willingness to kill Dumbledore by making an Unbreakable Vow with Bellatrix's sister Narcissa Malfoy (during which he flinches only a little; after all, making an Unbreakable Vow should not be undertaken lightly). "'I have played my part well,'" Snape haughtily tells Bellatrix, and he's right (31). We may hate Snape when he kills Dumbledore, but there is something impressive, even majestic, about his icy poise, about the "revulsion and hatred etched in the harsh lines of his face" as he strikes down the Godlike father figure who trusted him (595). We have to respect Snape's commitment here; this is not a villain who does things by half-measures. This is not a coward, despite what Harry thinks.

During literature's Romantic age, Gothic novelists added a dash of Milton's Satan to the classic antagonist in black to create what we recognize as today's sympathetic villain. In spooky and supernatural Gothic novels like Horace Walpole's *The Castle of Otranto* (1764) and Ann Radcliffe's *The Italian* (1797), the villain is always dark-haired, unconventionally attractive, and cruel, but he has a shameful or tormented past that begs our sympathy. He is menacing, yet deeply charismatic. Radcliffe's description of her villainous monk Schedoni in *The Italian* could apply to Snape himself: "Among his associates, no one loved him, many disliked him and more feared him. His figure was striking . . . and as he stalked along, wrapped in the black garment of his order, there was something terrible in its air . . . An habitual gloom and severity prevailed over the deep lines of his countenance, and his eyes were so piercing that they seemed to penetrate, at a single glance, into the hearts of men and to read their most secret thoughts" ("The Satanic and Byronic Hero: Texts and Contexts," Norton Topics Online). Does the word "severity" leap out at you? It should.

## So Bad They're Good

Like the Gothic villains, Snape is irresistibly over-the-top in his sinister and detestable behavior. After all, there are few character-types more loathesome than the mean teacher—and Snape is the mean teacher who also kills Santa Claus. But even though she gives us plenty of reasons to hate him, Rowling still stops short of characterizing Snape as truly evil. In *Half-Blood Prince*, she has Dumbledore make an important distinction between Snape and the young Voldemort, Tom Riddle—Dumbledore

trusts Snape, but he tells Harry that he never overestimated Riddle's trustworthiness. Dumbledore saw the warning signs of Riddle's evil nature (his alarming cruelty and lack of conscience) when he was still a child. But he saw no such signs in Snape when he was a student at Hogwarts. Even more meaningful is the statement that Rowling places in the mouth of her surrogate in the books, Hermione, who is usually right about everything. "'Evil' is a strong word,'" Hermione cautions Harry when he uses this word to describe Snape in the aftermath of Dumbledore's death (638). Rowling is telling us here that we should not place Snape at the top of the villain food chain. That dubious honor belongs to the grotesque Voldemort, who is the personification of pure evil in the saga.

Snape is, instead, a masterful example of a bad guy to whom we can secretly relate. That's in part due to the humanizing touches Rowling has given him—the humiliation, the loneliness, the underpants. Who's to say how any of us would have turned out when faced with the torment and hurt Snape went through? As humans, we are attracted to villains as a way of safely confronting and exploring our own dark side—the road not taken. There are limits to how far this exploration should go, though; not many of us (hopefully) would feel comfortable wearing a Hitler costume on Halloween. And it would be nice to imagine that, given Snape's options, not many of us would choose to become a Death Eater, either. But, within the pretend world of books and movies, Snape is the type of complicated, magnetic, sympathetic villain who turns a simple tale of good-vs.-evil into something more provocative. He confuses our loyalties, seduces us. We know we should hate him, reject him, but there's a little part of us—the bad little part of us—that feels a shiver of admiration for his wickedness.

The select group of fascinating—at times, even oddly heroic—villains to which Snape belongs is headed by Darth Vader, of course. But the list also includes charismatic villains as varied as the Wicked Witch of the West in *The Wizard of Oz*, Captain Hook in *Peter Pan* (especially Jason Isaacs's sympathetic Hook in the 2003 movie), Anthony Hopkins's Hannibal Lecter in *Silence of the Lambs*, Gollum in Lord of the Rings, the microscopic of stature but toweringly ambitious Plankton on *SpongeBob SquarePants*, the Sheriff of Nottingham in the movie *Robin Hood: Prince of Thieves*, and Hans Gruber in *Die Hard*. (The tantrum-prone Sheriff and the suave Hans Gruber—both scene-stealers—were

played by none other than Alan Rickman, Snape of the Harry Potter movies.)

What is it about these iconic villains that blurs good and bad, makes us admire (if not openly root for) treachery, cruelty, and mayhem? In the case of movie villains, it has a lot to do with the ability some fine actors have to connect with and embody our own dark wishes, to act out our wicked impulses so we don't have to. But from a storytelling standpoint, a hero can't fulfill his destiny without a villain. To paraphrase Sacha Baron Cohen's Jean Girard, the charming French antagonist to Will Ferrell's redneck NASCAR driver in *Talladega Nights: The Ballad of Ricky Bobby*, "God needs ze Devil and ze Beatles needed ze Rolling Stones." The purpose of the villain is to be a worthy adversary, to test the hero. And make no mistake about it, we love to see our heroes tested. We love to see them suffer and almost fail; we're not just going to hand them our respect, we want them to earn it. And we love underdogs who come back from the brink of disaster, whether they're heroes or villains.

What else makes a great villain? With movie villains, you can't underestimate the importance of great visuals. What would Star Wars be without Darth Vader in that fearsome helmet and cape? What would *Silence of the Lambs* be without Dr. Lecter's creepy bite-restraining face mask? Which *Die Hard* fashion statement do you prefer—John McClane's dirty, ripped undershirt, or Hans Gruber's immaculately tailored suit? Who's funnier, the exuberantly twisted Dr. Evil or the kinda boring Austin Powers? The Snape of the movies is like a playlist of charismatic villain greatest hits. Like Darth Vader, he's got the coolness of a basic black wardrobe going for him, and he's got the deep, authoritative voice, too. Like Dr. Evil, not to mention Count Olaf of *Lemony Snicket's A Series of Unfortunate Events*, Snape makes us laugh intentionally (as in *Goblet of Fire*, when he repeatedly smacks Harry and Ron in the head with perfect slapstick timing). Like Hannibal the Cannibal, Snape makes us laugh nervously (as in *Sorcerer's Stone*, when his black eyes bore a hole through Harry, Ron, and Hermione as he tells them to stop sneaking around or people might think they're up to something). And, like Hans Gruber and the Sheriff, he's Alan Rickman. Villainy doesn't get much better than Snape.

# Speculations

## What Is Snape's Secret Vice?

Dumbledore craves candy. Trelawney drinks. Does Snape have any vices—well, besides Dark magic, spying on people, and tormenting students? The Potions Master is such a man of mystery in every aspect of his life that there has to be a juicy little bad habit buried in all that darkness. But he never even appears to be having any fun. Food doesn't seem to excite him; we never see him actually eating at any of the tempting feasts in the Hogwarts dining hall. He doesn't seem overly fond of alcohol, either; he drinks some elf-made wine in the "Spinner's End" chapter of *Half-Blood Prince*, but he doesn't get plastered. At the Yule Ball in *Goblet of Fire*, he doesn't dance or chat up any of the female staff, preferring to roam the grounds catching couples making out. Internet chat rooms? Pfft—filled with Muggles. Video games? Bah—who needs *Halo* when you have a wand? Drugs? Well, he *is* the Potions Master. However, his absolute adherence to rules and regulations, and his uptight attitude toward, well, everything, makes it highly improbable that he'd ever engage in such a reckless activity. Not only does Snape dress like a Puritan minister, he acts like one.

So where does Snape turn for a mindless diversion at the end of a long day of rage and paranoia? What is the guilty pleasure to which he surrenders behind the heavy locked doors of his dungeon apartment at Hogwarts? What opiate carries him away into the oblivion of pure gratification? Four words: *Dancing. With. The. Stars.*

### The Two Faces of Snape

The truest test of great villains is whether you're sad to see them go. When Hans Gruber falls out that thirty-story window, when the Wicked Witch melts, when Darth Vader sacrifices himself to save Luke from the Dark Side, they leave an undeniable void. We know they had to be vanquished, even deserved it, but still, we have to catch our breath and reflect on the tragic waste of all that brilliance, ambition, and style. When a bad guy's demise stirs up this sort of reaction, it's proof of how closely the sympa-

thetic villain and the misunderstood hero are related. Sometimes, a character is both at the same time. Anakin Skywalker begins as a tragic antihero and ends as Darth Vader, sympathetic villain. In killing the Emperor to save his son, Vader acknowledges the flicker of humanity that still lives inside him. Snape could well be both innocent and guilty, hero and villain. And he could be headed for a Vaderesque fate.

Snape displays all the signs of being a type of character known as a Shapeshifter, whose purpose is to add both doubt and suspense to a story.[1] The Shapeshifter starts out as good, bad, or neutral and switches sides at a crucial point; often, the hero is not certain of his loyalties until the last minute. The questions to ponder about Snape the Shapeshifter are when and why he shifted allegiances, assuming he did truly work for Dumbledore at some point. Shapeshifters who switch from good to bad, like Cypher in *The Matrix* and Judas in the Gospels, are unable to resist temptation; they succumb to their weaknesses and betray the hero. Snape the sympathetic villain has his weaknesses just like everyone else. What could have made him betray Dumbledore? Were Snape's thirty pieces of silver the fame, glory, and immortality he spoke of back in that first Potions class? Or was his price simply the chance to avenge his long-ago humiliation, the chance to destroy that small voice in his head that tells him he is weak and a coward? Snape has made his bargain with evil; now he has to live with himself. Or will he, like Darth Vader, be swayed by that tiny remainder of his better nature at the end?

Snape's shame, as represented by the debacle of the graying underpants, is the key to his personality; how he chooses to deal with this shame will determine his ultimate fate in the saga. The shame makes Snape tragic, unpredictable, and, above all, human. Unlike Voldemort, Snape has not (as far as we know) torn apart his soul. He is not a monster, he is a man—personally flawed, perhaps even as sinister as he appears to be, but still a man. Snape is the most intriguing kind of villain, the one who reminds us that we all carry the seeds of good and evil within us. Some of us just hide our Dark Marks better than others.

---

[1] You can read more about Snape as Shapeshifter in "In Defense of Snape," in the other half of this book.

# III.
# THE LIFE OF
# SEVERUS SNAPE:
# ROTTEN TO THE CORE

THE VILLAINOUS SEVERUS SNAPE was born on January 9th, and shares his birthday with Richard Nixon, American serial killer Dorothea Puente, and Mehmet Ali Agca (the Turkish would-be assassin of Pope John Paul II). His mother was Eileen Prince, a pure-blooded witch who, unsurprisingly, attended Hogwarts at approximately the same time as Tom Riddle and who looked "simultaneously cross and sullen, with heavy brows and a long, pallid face" (*Half-Blood Prince* 537). The hook-nosed and thoroughly unpleasant Tobias Snape, a Muggle, was his hot-tempered and abusive father.

Living with cruel and neglectful parents in a filthy house, the juvenile Severus was a miserable and isolated child completely lacking social skills. Instead of finding beneficial or constructive ways to cope with his unhealthy home life, as Harry Potter did with the Dursleys, he took out his repressed emotions in harmful ways, using destructive magical talents to kill small creatures while bored in his room—an action reminiscent of the young Voldemort.

When he reached the appropriate age, Snape attended Hogwarts School of Witchcraft and Wizardry for his education in magic. Even as early as his very first year, Snape possessed an abnormally strong fascination with the Dark Arts, just as Tom Riddle did when he arrived at the school. In fact, Snape knew more Dark spells in his first year at Hogwarts than most seventh-year students did. Appropriately sorted into Slytherin upon arrival at Hogwarts, the House known for its lack of ethics and its focus on achieving goals by any means necessary, he soon found common ground with an older student: a future key Death Eater named Lucius Malfoy. Malfoy took Snape under his wing and inducted him into his circle of Slytherin friends, the members of which all later involved themselves heavily in the Dark Arts and pledged their loyalty to Voldemort.

Snape's contemporaries at Hogwarts also included five well-known students who would—except for one—faithfully serve the side of good: James Potter and Lily Evans, Sirius Black, Remus Lupin, and the turncoat Peter Pettigrew, all of whom resided in the rival Gryffindor House. The four boys formed a group known as the Marauders, and the unpopular teenage Snape was often at odds with these admired Gryffindor students.

As Sirius once explained to Harry, "'James and Snape hated each other from the moment they set eyes on each other, it was just one of those

things, you can understand that, can't you? I think James was everything Snape wanted to be—he was popular, he was good at Quidditch, good at pretty much everything. And Snape was just this little oddball who was up to his eyes in the Dark Arts and James . . . always hated the Dark Arts'" (*Order of the Phoenix* 670). Lupin added in the same conversation that Snape "'never lost an opportunity to curse James'" (671). In fact, although Snape is often painted as a victim by those who don't want to see the man's villainy. Snape was, in fact, perfectly capable of defending himself and did so, sometimes violently, as when Snape used the Dark spell *Sectumsempra* on James ("But too late; Snape had directed his wand straight at James; there was a flash of light and a gash appeared on the side of James's face, spattering his robes with blood'" (*Order of the Phoenix* 647).

Snape's skill at brewing potions, no matter how vile or odorous, nearly matched his skill at the Dark Arts. Unsatisfied by the standard, mundane course work, he developed alternate methods of brewing many of the potion recipes traditionally taught at Hogwarts, giving him an edge on his fellows who followed the recipe, thus cheating his way to the top of the class. He recorded these adjusted instructions in his Potions textbook, a book that Harry later discovered. Snape also used the book's margins to record a number of Dark spells (such as the harmful aforementioned *Sectumsempra*, translated from Latin as "cuts forever").

Snape wrote "Property of the Half-Blood Prince" in this textbook, a title that referred to both his half-Muggle bloodline and his mother's name. Snape's nickname for himself is reminiscent of Lord Voldemort's own; much like Tom Riddle, another half-blood who never believed that he was ordinary, the teenage Snape styled himself as nobility, discarding the name of his Muggle father just as Riddle did.

During Snape's fifth year, just after he'd sat for his O.W.L.s, James Potter rightfully paid him back for some of the Dark curses he'd received from the Slytherin boy over the years by hanging him upside-down—a harmless prank that took on a greater significance in Snape's mind, inflaming his anger and strengthening his already unhealthy desire for revenge.

Another prank set up by the Marauders cemented that desire. Sirius Black, whose dislike for Snape was no secret, attempted to trap him with fellow Marauder Lupin, a werewolf, during the full moon. At the last minute, James stopped Snape from falling for Sirius's ploy, realizing that,

in their boyish enthusiasm, they had crossed the line. Despite the fact that James had both saved his life and betrayed one of his fellow Marauders to do so, Snape, knowing James was involved in the plot, never forgave either him or Sirius.

James Potter went on to become Head Boy of Hogwarts in his seventh year, leading the student body with a mix of intelligence, magical ability, and spirit. Meanwhile, the sullen Snape bitterly remained alternately unnoticed or the object of scorn among his young peers.

Once he graduated from Hogwarts, Snape found the perfect way to utilize his formidable talents in the Dark Arts, as well as follow the example of his older Slytherin friends: he became a follower of Voldemort. He was welcomed among the ranks of the Death Eaters and within a few short years, he rose to become one of Voldemort's most trusted followers, faithfully serving the last surviving descendent of Salazar Slytherin for half a decade. During this time, he committed many unspeakable acts in the name of his lord and master.

As confirmation of his absolute loyalty, his colleagues branded him with the Dark Mark—the tattoo given to every Death Eater depicting a skull with a snake protruding from its mouth—on his lower left forearm. This mark appeared on every Death Eater whenever Voldemort summoned his followers, and it returned on Snape's arm fully after Voldemort's rebirth, an event that occurred long after he had claimed to have left the service of evil.

It was his role as a loyal Death Eater that led Snape to the Hog's Head Inn to seek a teaching job at Hogwarts. Snape was at that inn on the same night that Dumbledore interviewed Sybill Trelawney for the post of Divination professor, and he eavesdropped for his master just outside the door of Dumbledore's room when she made her legendary prophecy. Unfortunately for him, Snape only heard the first half of the prophecy before he was discovered and ousted from the inn. Snape rushed the information he had heard directly back to Voldemort, leading to deadly consequences.

Just prior to the Potters' deaths at Godric's Hollow, Snape went to Dumbledore and offered his services as a double agent and informer about the Death Eaters. Despite the fact that Voldemort was still at full power at that time, giving Snape no rational reason to change sides, Dumbledore didn't question the change of heart. Snape just appeared to be remorseful, and the trusting Dumbledore believed his story. Snape's

exceptional skills as an Occlumens hid his true intentions from Dumbledore and, possessing the complete (and easily won) trust of the headmaster, he was able to freely spy on his enemies at Hogwarts.

Dumbledore awarded Snape a teaching position, just as Voldemort had sent him to obtain. However, to Snape's frustration, he did not earn the position that he had sought. As Snape had an abundance of first-hand experience with Dark magic and long interest in the subject, he had hoped to teach Defense Against the Dark Arts in order to train new generations of Dark wizards and witches while pretending to teach them to defend against that aspect of their craft. However, despite his professed trust in Snape, Dumbledore quietly (and justly) feared that the Defense Against the Dark Arts position might bring out the worst in Snape's character.

Instead, Dumbledore offered him the position of Potions Master. Snape accepted the position, as it gave him a place at Hogwarts just as Voldemort had wished and protected him from well-earned prison time in Azkaban. However, he made no secret of his desire to teach Defense Against the Dark Arts and reapplied for the position every year .(Hogwarts had gone through Defense Against the Dark Arts teachers rapidly since Tom Riddle was wisely denied the position).

After Voldemort's first defeat, the remaining Death Eaters were brought to trial by the Wizengamot. Snape, although denounced as a Death Eater by Igor Karkaroff, escaped serving time at Azkaban largely because the gullible Dumbledore spoke out in his favor. With Voldemort believed to be defeated and his cover story intact, Snape kept his post at Hogwarts, never deserting the position that Voldemort had ordered him to take and always hoping that he might one day teach Dark Arts to a new generation in Voldemort's memory. Consequently, throughout his years at Hogwarts, Snape continued to respectfully refer to Voldemort as his "Dark Lord."

For approximately the next fifteen years, Snape held the posts of both Potions Master and the head of Slytherin House at Hogwarts. As a teacher, Snape was merciless, unpleasant, nasty, and domineering to those in his charge, especially if they had been sorted to Gryffindor. He also developed a notorious reputation for favoring the students from his own House. Teaching deep in a dungeon so cold that students could see their own breaths during the winter, Snape kept students silent during class by his disposition alone, requiring little active effort from him in either discipline or teaching.

In 1991, Harry Potter started at Hogwarts. Snape immediately hated the boy for many reasons, but especially because he reminded him of his long-dead school adversary. Meanwhile, Draco Malfoy, the son of his old friend Lucius, quickly became his favorite student. In Harry's first class, Snape began what would become a tradition of torment as he quizzed Harry about potion facts he could not possibly know and blamed him for another student's mistakes. Throughout the year (and the years that followed) Snape tormented and belittled Harry and his friends, returning with interest the abuse he felt he had suffered at the hands of the Marauders. Ironically, Snape saved Harry from being cursed by Harry's first year Defense Against the Dark Arts teacher, Professor Quirrell, during a Quidditch match, and later refereed the Hufflepuff/Gryffindor Quidditch match so that Quirrell couldn't interfere a second time. But he did this largely to keep suspicion off himself in the eyes of the Hogwarts faculty, as, unlike the naïve Dumbledore, few of them trusted him. (Unsurprisingly, Dumbledore attributed Snape's actions to the more noble desire to fulfill the life debt he owed to James Potter.) What Snape did not realize was that Professor Quirrell, unbeknownst to the remaining loyal Death Eaters, had become a servant of Snape's Dark Lord after encountering the disembodied Voldemort in Albania.

It was Snape, not Quirrell, who became the object of Harry's suspicion early in the year when Harry, knowing that the hiding place of the Sorcerer's Stone was protected by a three-headed dog, noticed that Snape had been injured by some kind of animal. We later learned that the dog had bitten Snape when he tried to stop Quirrell from obtaining the Stone. Snape later told Narcissa Malfoy that he had tried to stop Quirrell because he did not think the man was worthy of the Sorcerer's Stone, and did not realize at the time that Voldemort was involved. Harry also overheard Snape in the forest as he threatened Quirrell, reminding him that no students were supposed to know about the Stone or what it was used for: creating a potion called the Elixir of Eternal Life.

Of course, an elixir like that would have been of great interest to Voldemort, and indeed it was, although Snape was not aware at the time that Voldemort was actively pursuing it. If he had been, his potion-making skills could have been of great help in making the elixir. It is entirely possible that Voldemort either erred by not confiding in his former student, or else planned to reveal himself after he was sure that Snape had remained loyal; with Snape's help, the

Dark Lord could have gained new power much sooner and, quite possibly, immortality.

At the end of the school year, Quirrell tried to obtain the Stone in order to bring Voldemort back to life, and thus Snape was cleared of all suspicions, although Harry still instinctively distrusted him.

In the next school year, Harry Potter again was an unenthusiastic student in Snape's required Potions class, and, even less happy about this arrangement, Snape continued both his constant point deductions from Gryffindor and his regular insults of Harry in particular. A reluctant participant in the dueling club begun by that year's Defense Against the Dark Arts professor, the inept Gilderoy Lockhart, Snape easily defeated Lockhart, then partnered Harry with his favorite, Draco, causing a nasty magic fight in which Snape advised Draco on how best to hurt the son of his old schoolyard nemesis. This battle exposed Harry as a Parselmouth, a rare skill he shared only with Lord Voldemort and Salazar Slytherin's other descendants. It was a skill, also, that made the entire school distrust him, given the rumors about Slytherin's heir and the Chamber of Secrets, and Parseltongue's association with Dark wizards. Thanks to Snape, Harry was suddenly ostracized by the entire school.

A backfired Memory Charm destroyed Lockhart's memory at the end of the school year, so the Defense Against the Dark Arts position opened up at Hogwarts once again. Denied the position yet again, Snape fought against the appointment of the new professor. His arguments failed, however, and Remus Lupin, secret werewolf and once-member of the Marauders, became the new Defense Against the Dark Arts professor. Lupin remained harmless so long as he drank a special Wolfsbane Potion every month, and as Snape already knew Lupin's secret, he reluctantly agreed to Dumbledore's request that he brew the Wolfsbane Potion for him; this turn of events put Snape into a position where he could manipulate the situation if the opportunity presented itself.

Near the end of the school year, that opportunity arrived: when Snape realized that Lupin had not taken his potion, he brought a goblet of it to Lupin's office, where he discovered the Marauder's Map, a magical object his childhood adversaries created in order to get away with their pranks. When Snape realized the map's purpose, it only fueled his hatred of the Marauders.

Based on what he saw on the map, he followed Lupin to the Shrieking Shack, also the hiding place of Snape's long-time enemy and Azkaban

escapee Sirius Black, who was falsely believed to have killed fellow Marauder Peter Pettigrew, the Potters, and several Muggle bystanders. But these horrible crimes meant little to Snape; more important was that Sirius was the one who had set up the childhood prank that Snape refused to forgive. Seeking revenge for all that he felt that the Marauders had done to him as a teenager and, ambitious as any Slytherin, hoping to earn the Order of Merlin for capturing the fugitive, Snape burst into the shack, triumphant and more than a little mad with vengeance. He threatened to summon the Dementors to destroy Sirius's soul rather than hear Sirius's defense, and even blustered that he would have Lupin incarcerated in Azkaban as well.

Before Snape was able to carry out his threats, Harry immobilized him to protect his innocent godfather. Snape did not learn the truth about Sirius until much later, but the man's innocence didn't matter much to Snape, nor did it erase the loathing Snape felt over everything he'd endured during school. Furious and bitter over Sirius's unexplained escape and his resultant loss of the Order of Merlin promised to him by Cornelius Fudge, Snape spitefully made public the fact that Lupin was a werewolf, forcing Lupin to resign from Hogwarts at the end of the school year before the outcry from concerned parents could begin.

As preparations for the historic Triwizard Tournament began the following fall, Snape's double life kept him in the background, where he remained for most of the school year. When he did appear, he continued to make Harry's life difficult in every way possible. He also continued his customary practice of committing petty acts of maliciousness; at the Yule Ball, he blasted rose bushes apart and handed detentions out liberally, reveling in the small amount of power that he wielded as a professor. He was also vocal in his belief that Harry himself was to blame for his name coming out of the Goblet of Fire, making Harry one of two Hogwarts Champions in the tournament even though the boy was technically too young to compete and magic barriers had been in place to prevent him from entering the competition. But Snape's protestations could as easily have been a cover for his knowledge about what was really going on— that year's Defense Against the Dark Arts teacher, the false Mad-Eye Moody, couldn't have pulled off Voldemort's whole scheme on his own, after all. When Voldemort returned to full life and power after the final round of the Triwizard Tournament, Snape was "summoned" to his Dark Lord's side via his Dark Mark, but he, along with Karkaroff (who, in fear,

fled the call), did not join the other Death Eaters in the graveyard right away. Instead, he chose to remain at first at Hogwarts, and to reveal his Dark Mark openly to Cornelius Fudge and the other wizards present in the hospital wing, ostensibly as an attempt to help Dumbledore prove that Voldemort had truly returned.

Of course, Snape had an ulterior motive in doing so: he couldn't hide his "past" affiliation, so he displayed the Dark Mark at a time that would help him avoid future suspicion, using this small piece of truth to create an even stronger lie. His action also had a convenient side effect. Voldemort's strength lay in sowing fear and discord, and such a revelation of the Dark Lord's return would only help his cause; as the events of the following year proved, few were willing to believe in the Dark Lord's return, but all feared it, whether they believed it or not.

After this "revelation," Dumbledore then asked Snape to take on a task that was all too easy considering his true allegiance: infiltrating the ranks of the Death Eaters. As Snape swept off, theoretically to do Dumbledore's bidding, even Dumbledore, with all his supposed trust in Snape, couldn't hide the apprehension on his face now that Snape was free at long last to go to the side of his Dark Lord and take his rightful place among the Death Eaters—with Dumbledore's ill-considered blessing and without losing his enemies' trust. The following summer, Snape became a member of the newly reformed Order of the Phoenix, an organization created solely to fight Voldemort and his followers. Sadly, Dumbledore believed that Snape gathered information *for* the Order, not on the Order.

With the false Mad-Eye Moody unmasked and the real Mad-Eye Moody concentrating on fighting Voldemort and his Death Eaters, the Defense Against the Dark Arts post re-opened, but Dumbledore again denied Snape the position, despite the fact that the only alternative was to have the Ministry of Magic force its own choice of teacher upon Hogwarts. Snape must not have fought very hard for the position this year; he already had a full plate between keeping up his Order cover and gathering information for Voldemort. He quietly retained his Potions class and stayed out of the way of Ministry appointee Dolores Umbridge, as the discord she sowed in the school was of use to Voldemort's cause. He only took action when he knew that not doing so would expose him as less than a "loyal" teacher and member of the Order.

On Dumbledore's orders, Snape began teaching Harry about Occlumency every Monday and Wednesday. Dumbledore had hoped that

these lessons would help Harry better protect his mind from Voldemort and his followers, but the headmaster picked the wrong teacher for the job. After the first lesson, Harry couldn't help thinking that the experience had weakened his mind's resistance instead of strengthening it against intrusion. He left each lesson shivering and feeling almost feverish. Snape undermined Harry's mental defenses right under everyone's noses. His friends and mentors encouraged him to continue, even though Harry's instincts warned otherwise. Thanks to Snape and his "lessons," Harry's dreams about Voldemort became stronger and stronger, and his link with Voldemort seemed to increase as the lessons progressed.

> Before he had started studying Occlumency, his scar had prickled occasionally, usually during the night, or else following one of those strange flashes of Voldemort's thoughts or moods that he experienced every now and then. Nowadays, however, his scar hardly ever stopped prickling, and he often felt lurches of annoyance or cheerfulness that were unrelated to what was happening to him at the time, which were always accompanied by a particularly painful twinge from his scar. He had the horrible impression that he was slowly turning into a kind of an aerial that was tuned in to tiny fluctuations in Voldemort's mood, and he was sure he could date this increased sensitivity firmly from his first Occlumency lesson with Snape (*Order of the Phoenix* 553-554).

Snape also exhausted and humiliated Harry during each of his Occlumency attempts. When Harry asked why Snape still referred to Voldemort as the "Dark Lord"—"'I've only ever heard Death Eaters call him that—'" Harry challenged (*Order of the Phoenix* 593)—he dodged the question. During one lesson, Harry witnessed Snape's "worst memory" in the Pensieve: James Potter tormenting a young and humiliated Snape by hanging him upside down. Snape ended the lessons angrily, upset that Harry had learned of his old shame and disturbed, no doubt, that he could possibly uncover more—like information that could expose him for who he really is.

Near the end of the term, Harry and his friends followed his Snape-strengthened visions to "save" Sirius as part of a trap set by Voldemort, one that led the Death Eaters straight to the prophecy about himself and Harry. Fortunately, the prophecy was destroyed in the battle, and there

was only one casualty on the side of good. And although Sirius was the one killed, Snape was not able to be present to witness the death of his long-time enemy.

Dumbledore believed that Snape saved many lives when he alerted the Order that Harry had gone to the Department of Mysteries. However, had Snape not contacted the Order about Harry's plans, Harry (had he survived) could have exposed him for what he really was; *not* alerting the Order would have blown his cover. Snape had also repeatedly goaded Sirius about remaining safely at Grimmauld Place during battles, egging him on to join the battle with the Death Eaters, and so Harry rightfully blamed Snape for his part in his godfather's death.

That summer, Narcissa Malfoy and Bellatrix Lestrange visited Snape at his home at Spinner's End. Narcissa knew that Snape was the Dark Lord's favorite, but sister Bellatrix, recently fallen out of favor with Voldemort herself and no doubt jealous of Snape's position within the Death Eater ranks, still doubted, and interrogated him about his actions and motivations. Snape responded easily to every question she posed, detailing his loyalty throughout the years and how his tireless efforts had all been for the glory of his Dark Lord. His strategy of staying in the shadows and remaining at Hogwarts had ultimately allowed him to move into prime position to serve Voldemort. They also discussed the recently deceased Emmeline Vance, a member of the Order who was "nastily" murdered by Death Eaters; during this conversation, Snape revealed to Bellatrix that he was the one who betrayed the stout-hearted witch, giving the Death Eaters yet another victory.

Narcissa feared for her son Draco because of the difficult task Voldemort had assigned him to carry out, and for good reason: the boy had been tasked to kill Dumbledore. Snape believed that Draco had been set up to fail by the Dark Lord because of Lucius's failure to retrieve the prophecy and his subsequent capture, but Snape, with no doubt years of anger and resentment built up toward the men, had every reason to want Draco to succeed. At Narcissa's plea, Snape agreed to assist his favorite student in fulfilling his task, and take it up should Draco falter. Snape then cemented his promise by accepting Narcissa's request to make an Unbreakable Vow, obligating him to watch over Draco "'as he attempts to fulfill the Dark Lord's wishes,'" to "'protect [Draco] from harm,'" and to "'carry out the deed that the Dark Lord has ordered Draco to perform'" if it seemed that Draco would fail (*Half-Blood Prince* 36).

Following Umbridge's departure at the end of the school year, Dumbledore gave Snape the job that he had sought at Hogwarts for so long: teaching Defense Against the Dark Arts. Although preparations to teach the Dark Arts to a new generation certainly took up a great deal of his time, Snape still volunteered to meet Harry, late to the welcome feast thanks to Draco's vicious abuse on the train to Hogwarts, at the gate on the first evening of the new school year, and, after spitefully deducting points from Gryffindor for Harry's tardiness, sent him into the Great Hall alone with his nose broken and his clothing covered in his own blood.

Snape, relishing his new teaching position, waxed poetic about his favorite subject during his first class with the sixth-year students: "'The Dark Arts . . . are many, varied, ever-changing, and eternal. Fighting them is like fighting a many-headed monster, which, each time a neck is severed, sprouts a head even fiercer and cleverer than before. You are fighting that which is unfixed, mutating, indestructible'" (*Half-Blood Prince* 177). He also attempted to hit Harry with a jinx in that initial class simply out of spite, but Harry retaliated.

Later in the term, Snape discovered that Harry had unwittingly used Snape's own dangerous *Sectumsempra* spell on Draco, a Dark spell which Harry had found in Snape's old Potions book. This spell, an early Snape original, cuts its victim cruelly and resists non-magical healing. Snape, furious that Harry would dare to use his spell and that his favorite student was hurt by it—even though Draco had been about to cast the unforgivable Cruciatus Curse on Harry, and Harry had acted only in self-defense, not even knowing what the spell did—gave Harry detention for the rest of the school year. Snape realized then that Harry learned this Dark and dangerous spell from his old textbook.

Snape attempted to convince Draco to let him assist with his task of killing the Hogwarts headmaster, a man under whom Snape had bitterly toiled in a dungeon as Potions Master for more than fifteen years, a wizard who he had to pretend to admire while being denied the Defense Against the Dark Arts position year after year, a man who, worst of all, was the primary thorn in the side of his Dark Lord. After suffering so many indignities, even aside from the benefits it would provide to Voldemort's cause, Snape doubtlessly wanted Dumbledore dead.

By the end of the school year, Draco had devised a way to bring Death Eaters into Hogwarts, and found himself facing a poisoned Dumbledore at the top of the Astronomy Tower. Snape rushed onto the scene to find

Draco faltering, unable to complete the task given to him. Dumbledore, clearly believing in Snape's story of remorse even to the last, said, "'Severus . . . please . . . ,'" in a pleading voice but Snape ignored the headmaster's plea for mercy and then, with "revulsion and hatred etched in the harsh lines of his face" murdered Dumbledore with the Unforgivable Curse *Avada Kedavra*, utterly destroying him (*Half-Blood Prince* 595).

Snape fled the tower as soon as the deed was done, rushing with Draco back into the castle, past the ongoing battle and out to a place where he would be able to escape, but Harry, having been witness to the whole scene, pursued him. Once out on the grounds of the school, Harry caught up with Dumbledore's killer, but Snape easily blocked every curse that Harry cast and even went so far as to taunt him by telling him what he was doing wrong. "'You dare use my own spells against me, Potter? It was I who invented them—I, the Half-Blood Prince! And you'd turn my inventions on me, like your filthy father, would you? I don't think so . . . *no!*'" (*Half-Blood Prince* 604). Despite no doubt being tempted himself, Snape adhered strictly to his master's orders and stopped one of his fellow Death Eater from casting the unforgivable Cruciatus Curse on Harry, reminding him that the boy belonged to their Dark Lord. He then Disapparated and went on the run, free to openly stand alongside his brother and sister Death Eaters at long last. The criminal's whereabouts are currently unknown.

## A Perverseness for Soups
### Fun with Anagrams

By now, most Harry Potter fans have played the anagram game. J. K. Rowling's love of wordplay and puzzles has some people convinced that she's hiding clues in characters' names, which can be discovered with a little rearrangement and a lot of creative interpretation. The most famous Harry Potter anagram is "Perseus Evans," which is what you get when you shuffle the letters of "Severus Snape." "Evans" is, of course, Lily Potter's maiden name. Is Snape a long-lost brother? It all fits! Um, just ignore all that important stuff about Snape's parentage from *Half-Blood Prince*.

The lore surrounding the name "Perseus" is more genuinely provocative. In Greek mythology, Perseus, a son of Zeus, slays the Medusa, whose hair is made of snakes (the Slytherin connection) and who has the power to turn those who look at her face into stone (like the Basilisk in *Chamber of Secrets*). Perseus' grandfather Acrisius is told by the Oracle that he will be killed by his grandson. Years later, Perseus does indeed kill his grandfather—accidentally (discus, high wind). Snape didn't kill his grandfatherly protector Dumbledore with a discus, and it didn't appear to be accidental. But, in light of the Perseus myth, it's worth revisiting Dumbledore's plea of "'Severus . . . please,'" a moment before Snape raises his wand. Did Dumbledore, like Acrisius, know far in advance of his death who his killer would be?

A visit to the Internet Anagram Server (http://www.wordsmith.org/) revealed these additional reshufflings of "Severus Snape":

SAVE PURENESS (Okay, we'll buy that.)
SUAVENESS REP (Are you kidding? Snape is the poster boy for suave! Oh, wait—we're confusing him with Alan Rickman.)
SAVES PEN USER (Umbridge forced Harry to carve lines into his own hand with her special torture pen.)
PAUSES NERVES (Why, yes he does.)
SASS PEEVE RUN (Good advice if you plan on back-talking the Potions Master in his classroom.)

## A Perverseness for Soups (Con't.)
### *Fun with Anagrams*

When "Professor" was added to "Severus Snape," out came A PER-VERSENESS FOR SOUPS. Soups, potions—same thing. But the Anagram Server was just warming up. The phrase "Potions Master" released a torrent of eerily relevant anagrams.

The Anagram Server, it seems, is not a fan of Snape; PASTIEST MORON and A MONSTER I SPOT were two of its more coherent epithets. Apparently, the Anagram Server has not forgiven Snape for roughing up Harry when he caught him watching his worst memory in the Pensieve, either: MISTREAT SNOOP! IRATE STOMP SON!, it screamed. The Anagram Server was equally outspoken about Snape's motives: SNARE I TOM SPOT, it muttered sagely, proposing that Snape's ultimate goal is to depose Voldemort and become the new Dark Lord.

Food for thought, wise Anagram Server, food for thought.

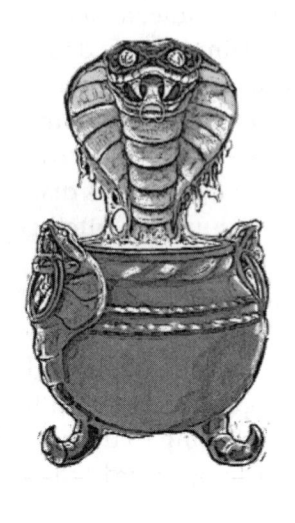

# IV.
# ALAN RICKMAN:
# THE VILLAIN
# CHARACTER EXPERT

ALAN RICKMAN IS A WICKEDLY GOOD ACTOR, and each of the villains he has created for stage or screen have been mesmerizing. An infamously corrupt sheriff, a manipulative Vicomte, a German pseudo-terrorist, a mad monk . . . Rickman takes villainy to new depths, often stealing the spotlight from the protagonist in the process. In the Harry Potter series, he commits the same sort of theft, his Snape joining his long list of tremendously evil characters. A September 1991 article in *GQ* summed him up perfectly: "Even his benevolent characters display hints of darkness, and his bad characters make evil sinuously intelligent and captivating."

## Villainous Stage and Television Roles

In 1973, at age twenty-six, Rickman applied for the Royal Academy of Dramatic Arts. The audition, which featured the first Rickman villain — Richard III — won him a scholarship to the school and, later, he also won his school's highest performing award, the Bancroft Medal. Clearly, Rickman was born to play jealous, ambitious characters like Richard and Snape.

He landed his first television role in 1978, appearing in a BBC adaptation of Shakespeare's *Romeo and Juliet* as the firebrand Tybalt, Juliet's cousin and a young man who constantly quarrels, never hesitating to draw a weapon in the face of an enemy. A few years later, Rickman appeared in another BBC adaptation: Anthony Trollope's *The Barchester Chronicles* (1982). As the Reverend Obadiah Slope, a sleazy, smarmy, and sinister politico, he manipulates this small-town, clergy-centric society to better his position any way he can.

Rickman played Hendrik Hofgen, another role that was appropriate for the actor who was to portray Snape, in the 1986 play *Mephisto*. This adaptation of the story of Mephistopheles and Doctor Faustus tells the tale of how the Faust-like main character, Hofgen, abandons his morals and conscience and curries favor with the Nazi Party in order to improve his job and social position.

The opportunity that made Rickman a star and propelled him to the big screen was the role of the heartless and manipulative Vicomte de Valmont in the play *Les Liaisons Dangereuses*. He originated the role in London, and then took it to Broadway, where he was nominated for a Tony (he was denied the role in the film adaptation, *Dangerous Liaisons*, in which the at the time better-known John Malkovich played the Vicomte).

## Die Hard

After his impressive turn as the Vicomte on Broadway, director John McTiernan tapped Rickman for his film debut: playing against Bruce Willis in a new, big-budget Hollywood offering, 1988's *Die Hard*. Although this film was meant to be a vehicle for Willis, Rickman matched him moment for moment, becoming as memorable in the film as the then-*Moonlighting* star. Between its two star actors and its exploding skyscraper, *Die Hard* easily became a blockbuster.

As German pseudo-terrorist Hans Gruber, Rickman exhibits many of Snape's central characteristics; Gruber is duplicitous, intelligent, well-educated ("'When Alexander saw the breadth of his domain, he wept for there were no more worlds to conquer.' The benefits of a classical education."), casually vicious, calculating, merciless, and driven. Although a former member of a terrorist organization, he has decided to use his skills and knowledge for personal gain instead. With a comfortable cover built from pieces of his past, he acts as a typical terrorist in order to mislead the authorities, blowing up a skyscraper in order to hide his true goal of stealing $640 million from the building's high-security vault. He hides his clever plan behind bogus requests that "revolutionaries" who, in truth, he only knew about from television, be freed. He also masquerades as a hostage when confronted by the hero of the piece, John McClaine. Gruber is also a master of large- and small-scale misdirection, using false assumptions and official procedures to his own advantage.

Rickman's portrayal won more than critical and popular acclaim. In 2003, the American Film Institute named Hans Gruber as the forty-sixth greatest villain in the past 100 years of film.

## Robin Hood: Prince of Thieves

Although much of 1991's *Robin Hood: Prince of Thieves* is forgettable, Alan Rickman's Sheriff of Nottingham is not; Rickman's performance remains the most memorable facet of the film. Quotes from his gloriously wicked version of this infamous character stay with you: "Wait a minute . . . Robin Hood steals money from my pocket, forcing me to hurt the public, and they love him for it? That's it then. Cancel the kitchen scraps for lepers and orphans, no more merciful beheadings, and call off

Christmas." As the hated Sheriff, Rickman treats us to some quality excessive evil. Let's not forget his desire to cut out Robin Hood's heart with a spoon. Why a spoon? "Because it's DULL, you twit. It'll hurt more." Extreme villains are always the most fun.

According to a June 1991 article in *Entertainment Weekly*, after one of the film previews, "When people were asked their favorite character, they picked not Costner's Robin but Rickman's Sheriff. While Costner had been robbing from the rich, Rickman had been stealing the movie." Sadly, this response worried the producers as Costner was their star, and so they brought in their own team of editors to pare down Rickman's screen time, angering the director, who walked off the project because of it.

## Rasputin

Perhaps it was his role as the infamous monk Rasputin, a performance for which he won a Golden Globe and an Emmy in 1996, which best reflects Rickman's depiction of Severus Snape. This real-life "mad monk" (who wasn't actually a monk; he had a family in Siberia) ensconced himself with the Russian nobility, in particular the Czar Nicholas II and his wife, Czarina Alexandra, after claiming to have cured their son. Describing the telepic, the *New York Times* wrote on March 23, 1996, "Sympathy for the devil has rarely been carried to such a delirious extreme as it is in *Rasputin*, an HBO movie with Alan Rickman exquisitely cast as the mystic who captured the minds of the doomed, imperial Romanovs. Shaggy-haired and laser-eyed, this Rasputin has manic energy, raw sexuality and extremely bad table manners." *Variety* called Rickman's performance "stunning," going on to say in a March 1996 article that, "Rickman's electric Rasputin seizes attention with the actor's magnetism and dramatic know-how."

Rasputin's story reflects themes similar to those found in Snape's as well: power, manipulation, and misplaced trust. Rasputin quietly gathered power, taking advantage of opportunities his situation provided and then manipulating events to get the Czar out of the way in order to take greater control of the country: he claimed that he had a vision in which he saw that the Russian armies would not be successful until the Czar personally took command. Although unprepared for the task, Nicholas proceeded to take personal command of the Russian army, resulting in dire consequences for himself and for Russia. While the Czar was away

at the front, Rasputin's influence over the Czarina increased; he quickly became her confidant and personal advisor. He convinced her to fill some government offices with his own handpicked candidates. As the Czarina was of German descent, members of the court accused Rasputin of being a spy in German employ. The legends of his death almost make him seem a wizard himself; as the legend goes, he was poisoned, shot, stabbed, beaten, and, lastly, drowned before he finally died; his reported ability to cheat death makes him seem far more than a mere Muggle.

## Other Notable Roles

The list of Rickman's other villains ranges from the delightfully over-the-top to the disturbingly real. From Angelo in *Measure for Measure* to Elliott Marston in *Quigley Down Under*, to King Philip Motzinger in the episode "Joust Like a Woman" of *King of the Hill*, Rickman creates antagonists better than anyone working today. But two of his other villains also deserve special attention.

In *Bob Roberts*, Tim Robbins's political satire, Rickman plays Lukas Hart III, the campaign's devious campaign manager. "The people behind candidates tend to be transparent," said Robbins in a 1992 interview in *Lear's Magazine*. "I was interested in casting someone who was a cross between Dr. Strangelove and William Casey. I don't like safe actors, which is why I chose Alan, who has the courage to make bold choices and chew on the scenery a little bit. He's also got a whimsy to him when he plays evil that's very seductive. I'd like to play opposite him in a movie about competing psychopaths. I'd like to try and out-psychopath Alan Rickman."

1996 brought us *Michael Collins*, in which Rickman plays American-born Sinn Fein President Eamon de Valera, a politician who seems to spend more time out of the country than in it. In his absence, Collins leads the struggle for Irish independence, gaining an uncomfortable amount of power. De Valera sends Collins to negotiate with the ruling British after years of bloody conflict, making him take the fall for a compromise that, while necessary, he knew his countrymen would hate. De Valera then usurps Collins's power base, which leads to the Irish hero's death by stoning.

*Time* lauded him for his role in October 1996: "[De Valera is] wonderfully played by Alan Rickman as a deeply devious neurasthenic, but he

is seen by Jordan as the kind of political sophisticate who has been betraying simple-hearted soldiers of rebellion since Errol Flynn (or maybe Douglas Fairbanks Sr.) was a pup."

## The Future

As of this writing, Rickman is slated to portray the depraved villain Judge Turpin in Tim Burton's big-screen adaptation of Stephen Sondheim's musical *Sweeney Todd: The Demon Barber of Fleet Street*. A despicable character who holds a high position in town, Turpin sends Todd to jail on a trumped-up charge to get him out of the way, then rapes and destroys his wife, raises his daughter as his ward and tries to marry her, then sends her to an asylum when those plans are interrupted. Turpin's respectable, polished exterior hides the blackest of hearts, just as Snape's story of remorse hides his true loyalties from Dumbledore, and Turpin is the target of Todd's revenge, which sets the entire dark plot of the main story in motion. Will Harry's wish to avenge Dumbledore's death set him on a destructive path in the final book as well? We'll just have to hope that Harry doesn't start cooking people into pies.

# Speculations

## Why Is Snape's Hair So Greasy?

**Dear Beauty Editor:**

I am a forty-ish male who is currently in a very stressful situation, both personally and career-wise. I have always had rather oily hair, no matter how much I wash it, but lately, one could prepare a batch of fish and chips in the residue left upon my morning pillow. Can stress make one's hair greasier? I have used various herbal potions, to no avail. Are there any ~~Muggle~~ conventional remedies that I can try?

—S. S.

**Dear S. S.:**

Plenty of things can add up to lank locks: bad genes, careless personal hygiene, over-active hormones, and, yes, stress. Greasy hair is caused by a build-up of the natural secretions from sebaceous glands in the scalp. Not washing the hair enough makes the problem worse. Be faithful about shampooing every day. Clairol Herbal Essences Fruit Fusions Purifying Shampoo is a fun choice. Or splurge on Matrix Biolage Normalizing Shampoo, followed by Tisserand Tea Tree Conditioner. Greasiness is especially noticeable on short hair, because the grease has less of a surface over which to spread. So, hopefully, you're already letting your hair down in a flattering longer style like the one made popular by *American Idol's* Bo Bice.

The male hormone androgen, which can be boosted by stress, contributes to the activation of sebaceous glands. So be sure to get enough rest, eat healthily, and try to tone down some of the pressure in your life. Make time for relaxing soaks in a lavender-scented bath. Take a walk and admire the beauty around you. Sign up for a yoga class. And next time you're summoned to an urgent meeting with the boss and feel an oil slick starting to form on your scalp, just duck into the nearest bathroom and dab a little baby powder onto your roots. It works like magic!

# V.
# SLYTHERIN HOUSE:
# HOME FOR THE
# ETHICALLY
# CHALLENGED

SLYTHERIN IS ONE OF THE FOUR HOUSES of Hogwarts and the home of a quarter of the wizards and witches who attend the school. Salazar Slytherin, the founder of the House, believed in cunning, ambitious wizards who were of the purest blood, and he structured his House accordingly, going so far as to leave the school when his philosophies were questioned by fellow founder Godric Gryffindor. However, the questions were posed for good reason; such elitist and selfish tenets create a dangerous foundation for any organization.

The fact is that more Dark wizards and witches have come out of Slytherin House than any other. That shouldn't be a surprise; "Dark" magic is a powerful category, and those who the Sorting Hat sends to the halls of Slytherin are naturally drawn to power. Given their pragmatic natures, one wizard's evil could be another wizard's progress. Those in Slytherin are frank about their desire for success and will use any means necessary to attain it, whether they follow Voldemort or not.

But it's not just Slytherin ambition that marks them as evil. The Harry Potter books present a host of reasons to dislike and distrust the House. Consider the evidence.

### The Evils of Snakes

> Not by accident, you may be sure, do the Christian Scriptures make the father of knowledge a serpent—slimy, sneaking, and abominable.
>
> —H. L. MENCKEN, *Treatise on the Gods*, 1949

The symbol of Slytherin is the serpent, which is entirely appropriate to their philosophies. Snakes appear throughout the mythologies of ancient peoples, from Hercules' fight with the Hydra to Medusa's hairdo. Biblical references to the serpent abound, and the role of the creature in the Judeo-Christian creation story is perhaps the best-known serpent story on record (no matter how many books J. K. Rowling sells): the "cunning" serpent tempts Eve with the forbidden fruit of the Tree of Knowledge; she then tempts Adam with the fruit, thus causing them both to be kicked out of Eden. For his role in their transgression, the serpent was cursed to slither for all time: "And the Lord God said unto the serpent, because thou hast done this, thou art cursed above all cattle, and above every beast of the field; upon thy belly shalt thou go, and dust shalt thou eat all the days of thy life" (Genesis 3:14).

Serpents play vital roles in the entire Harry Potter series, mainly through their association with evil characters (with the possible exception of the boa constrictor Harry accidentally frees from the zoo in *Sorcerer's Stone*, perhaps foreshadowing his role in bringing Voldemort, the character most closely associated with snakes, back into full existence several books later). Voldemort's symbol, the Dark Mark, consists of a skull with a snake emerging from its mouth. The ability to speak to snakes in their own language, Parseltoungue, is generally considered to be one of the Dark Arts—unless your name is Harry Potter, of course. The only other known Parselmouths are the ancient Greek Dark wizard Harpo the Foul, Salazar Slytherin, and a few of Slytherin's direct descendants: Lord Voldemort, his grandfather Marvolo Gaunt, his mother Merope, and his uncle Morfin.

The Basilisk, a creature originally bred by Harpo the Foul and defeated by Harry in *Chamber of Secrets*, is a giant green serpent that seems to be the very embodiment of Slytherin. As the thousand-year-old story goes, Salazar Slytherin and Godric Gryffindor argued over whether to allow Muggle-born students into Hogwarts. It seems that Godric won the argument, as Slytherin then left the school, but not before building the Chamber of Secrets. The long-rumored (and thought to be fictional) Chamber was a secret room that housed the Basilisk, a monster that would fulfill Salazar's plan to purge Hogwarts of all those with impure (Muggle) blood. The legend also states that only the true heir of Slytherin can open the Chamber and release the monster within. That heir is none other than Tom Riddle, known in Harry's time as Lord Voldemort. And in *Chamber of Secrets*, Riddle fulfills the conditions of the legend by finding the Chamber and opening it, setting the Basilisk free to do Salazar's work.

The Chamber itself is a veritable shrine to Slytherin, from its snake-figured hidden opening at the second-floor bathroom sink to huge serpent carvings and a statue of Salazar himself. A wizard needs to speak Parseltongue to access the Chamber, something both Salazar and Riddle (and, of course, Harry) could speak.

A wizard such as this school founder, one who laid a trap to kill children like poor Myrtle and who would rather destroy people than let his school be "tainted," founded the House; the evil Voldemort is his "heir." Can we expect better from the House's other members?

The snake that we know best in the series is Nagini, the twelve-foot-long loyal pet of Voldemort. As a Parselmouth, Voldemort is capable of

communicating with her, but their bond seems to go beyond that: Nagini seems to be something like a magical familiar for Voldemort. While Voldemort was barely alive, his temporary body was sustained by Nagini's "milk," possibly referring to her venom (*Goblet of Fire* 7). After Voldemort returned to full strength, Nagini remained in his service, investigating on his behalf and killing on demand. Nagini also acts as the evil counterpart of Fawkes, Dumbledore's phoenix, as her venom hinders the healing process rather than accelerating it as Fawkes's tears do. (Of course, venom isn't usually all that good for any person's health anyway, wizard or Muggle.)

Dumbledore believed that Voldemort planned to create one of his seven Horcruxes from the power gained from Harry's murder, considering Harry's importance as "the Chosen One" foretold by Trelawney's prophecy. As that attempt is believed to have failed (unless Harry himself is a hidden Horcrux) Dumbledore believed that the murder of gardener Frank Bryce produced the final Horcrux and that—based on her behavior and the control Voldemort exerts over her—Nagini was its vessel.

As further evidence of this theory, Harry witnesses Nagini attacking Arthur Weasley in a dream from Nagini's point of view, as though his connection to Voldemort extends to his snake familiar ("'How come I saw through the snake's eyes,'" Harry asks in *Order of the Phoenix*, "'if it's Voldemort's thoughts I'm sharing?'" [532].) Certainly, as Dumbledore himself states, Nagini "underlines the Slytherin connection" with Voldemort, and that connection is unusually strong (*Half-Blood Prince* 506).

Of course, we can't talk about this green monster without talking about the "Green-Eyed Monster": jealousy. As Shakespeare wrote in act III, scene iii of *Othello*, "O! Beware, my lord, of jealousy; It is the green-eyed monster which doth mock the meat it feeds on." Green has long been considered the color of this unhealthy trait, one that members of Slytherin have in abundance, especially when faced with someone more intelligent than they are (such as Hermione), more famous (like Harry), or more respected (like Dumbledore). And green is, after all, Slytherin's House color.

## Blood Purity and Prejudices

> Because bigotry is probably the thing I detest most. All forms of intolerance, the whole idea of "that which is different from me is necessary evil." I really like to explore the idea that difference is equal and good.
>
> —J. K. Rowling, *Entertainment Weekly*, August 4, 2000

> "You place too much importance . . . on the so-called purity of blood! You fail to recognize that it matters not what someone is born, but what they grow to be!"
>
> —DUMBLEDORE, *Goblet of Fire* (708)

Slytherins believe that bloodline is of great importance and is a true measure of a wizard's magical ability, displaying prejudice and discrimination toward wizards who are not of "pure blood." To them, a wizard or witch with anything less than fully magical ancestry is automatically inferior. Some wizards even go so far as to taunt wizards who possess less-than-perfect bloodlines, insulting them by calling them "Mudbloods," a derogatory term that suggests "dirty" blood.

Membership in Slytherin often runs in the family: think of the Malfoys, the Lestranges, the Gaunts, the Crouches, the Notts, and the Blacks (Sirius excepted, of course). Slytherin House has had many respected (and pure-blooded) families on its rolls for generations, and normally tends to accept those with only the purest wizard blood.

Slytherin House discriminates by filling its ranks with those who have the best chance of success, and so, unless there is another good reason to sort a wizard in to the House, only those who are wizard-born are allowed in. Historically, with the exception of Voldemort himself, the most powerful wizards have had pure wizard blood in their veins, and those in Slytherin apparently like to keep the odds in their favor. The exclusion isn't personal. Officially.

Those who do not denounce those with "impure" blood are labeled as blood traitors, a derogatory term for pure-blooded wizards who do not maintain the proper prejudices against non-purebloods, whether Muggle or Muggle-born. This label is applied to the Weasley family, Sirius Black, Andromeda Tonks, and Albus Dumbledore.

Rowling compares these attitudes to the Nazis on her official site:

"The expressions 'pure-blood,' 'half-blood,' and 'Muggle-born' have been coined by people to whom these distinctions matter, and express their originators' prejudices. As far as somebody like Lucius Malfoy is concerned, for instance, a Muggle-born is as 'bad' as a Muggle. Therefore Harry would be considered only 'half' wizard, because of his mother's grandparents. If you think this is far-fetched, look at some of the real charts the Nazis used to show what constituted 'Aryan' or 'Jewish' blood. I saw one in the Holocaust Museum in Washington when I had already devised the 'pure-blood,' 'half-blood,' and 'Muggle-born' definitions, and was chilled to see that the Nazis used precisely the same warped logic as the Death Eaters. A single Jewish grandparent 'polluted' the blood, according to their propaganda."

Not all members of Slytherin, however, are of pure blood. In fact, two of its most prominent members are, in fact, half-bloods. Neither Tom Riddle nor Severus Snape is a pure-blooded wizard, of course, as each only possesses wizard blood on his mother's side, but each's talent and potential for tremendous power offset this, making each an asset to the House.

Snape possessed a cunning mind, natural aptitude for the Dark Arts, and brilliance at a wide variety of magic, ranging from Potions to Occlumency. And he had the raw talent that would force Slytherin to welcome him as a potential ally. As the years progressed, Snape became much more than a simple ally, eventually becoming Voldemort's "most trusted advisor," the head of Slytherin House, and the murderer of Albus Dumbledore.

Similarly, Tom Riddle, although descended from the esteemed Gaunt family and the last direct descendant of Salazar Slytherin himself, also had a Muggle father (who, along with his paternal grandparents, he murdered using the unforgivable Killing Curse while still a student at Hogwarts, setting up his uncle to take the blame). Despite this Slytherin-perceived shortcoming, the future Lord Voldemort excelled in the House of Slytherin, becoming a prefect and, eventually, Head Boy. Riddle excelled at everything he took on, becoming a favorite of his professors and gathering a group of followers, particularly fellow Slytherin students, to whom he referred as "friends" although he felt no real friendship toward them.

The power Riddle possesses as Voldemort is undeniable, by far the strongest of his generation and the generation that followed, and there-

fore many current and former Slytherin House members are drawn to him like a moth to flame. These wizards and witches, over-steeped in Slytherin tradition, fell in with Voldemort because of the power he wielded. If you want power more than anything, it only makes sense to ride the coattails of the most powerful wizard in recent memory. Is it right? No. But there we have the reason strong ambition is so often dangerous: People who are that driven to achieve their goals don't often take right and wrong into account.

### Famous Evil Slytherins throughout History

> "You'll soon find out that some wizarding families are better than others, Potter. You don't want to go making friends with the wrong sort. I can help you there."
> —DRACO MALFOY, *Sorcerer's Stone* (108)

Salazar Slytherin, the founder who favored wizards and witches of pure blood who were filled with ambition and cunning, set the tone for the House, ensuring through the Sorting Hat that it would always be filled with like-minded witches and wizards. We've already looked at Voldemort and Snape; how well do Salazar's other successors measure up?

The members of the House of Gaunt, direct descendants of Salazar Slytherin, were so concerned with maintaining their pure blood and their Slytherin lineage that they married almost exclusively within their own family. The continuous inbreeding and severe isolation led to a small family of disturbed individuals and, finally, Voldemort himself, who killed the Muggle side of his family and blamed it on his insane uncle.

The Bloody Baron is one if the earliest-known Slytherin members and is their official ghost. He is a forbidding, terrifying apparition covered with silvery bloodstains of unknown origin, although one theory is that he is covered in unicorn blood due to the silvery color. This ghost is the only one who can rein in the school poltergeist, Peeves, who calls him "Your Bloodiness" and "Mr. Baron."

One of the oldest and worst of the wizard families, the Noble and Most Ancient House of Black, has a long history in Slytherin. Most of them were blood purists; their family motto is *Toujours Pur* (French for "Always Pure"). They have made liberal use of the Dark Arts thoughout

their long history, and the Black family home (at 12 Grimmauld Place, which becomes the unlikely headquarters of the Order of the Phoenix), contains many dangerous artifacts. It also held a decorative tapestry into which the Black family tree is woven. Those who displease the family (like Sirius Black and Andromeda Black Tonks) are disowned and burned out of the tapestry by matriarch Walburga Black and her predecessors. Unsurprisingly, many in the Black clan thought that Voldemort was on the right track with his ideas about "purifying" the wizarding race, although some, including Sirius's parents, decided not to support him once they saw what he was willing to do for power, including killing fellow pure-bloods.

Some notable Blacks include Elladora Black, who started the family tradition of beheading their house-elves when they became too old to carry tea trays; Araminta Melliflua, a cousin of Walburga Black who tried to force a bill through the Ministry of Magic that would make Muggle-hunting legal; Phineus Nigellus Black, the most hated headmaster in Hogwarts history (Dolores Umbridge notwithstanding); and Bellatrix Black Lestrange, who, among many other atrocities, murdered her own cousin, Sirius.

The list of Death Eaters from Slytherin is long: Lucius Malfoy, Narcissa Black Malfoy, Evan Rosier, Walden MacNair (executioner for the Committee for the Disposal of Dangerous Creatures), and Bellatrix, Rodolphus, and Rabastan Lestrange (all of whom participated in the torture of Frank and Alice Longbottom, driving them to madness).

## Why You Don't Have to Be a Death Eater to Be Evil

There are, of course, Slytherins who didn't join the Death Eaters. But, as Sirius told Harry in *Order of the Phoenix*, the world isn't neatly divided into good people and Death Eaters; while it's true that not all members of Slytherin join the Death Eaters, it doesn't mean that all non-Death Eaters are automatically "good." Evil people can be against Voldemort and still be quite nasty in their own right.

The best example in Harry's world is Dolores Umbridge, the Senior Undersecretary to the Minister of Magic who was appointed Defense Against the Dark Arts teacher at Hogwarts, High Inquisitor of the school, and then (temporarily) headmistress, and who Stephen King called in a 2003 issue of *Entertainment Weekly* the "greatest make-believe

villain to come along since Hannibal Lecter." Umbridge likely spent her school years in Slytherin (although it is never explicitly stated that Umbridge was a Slytherin, she does fill her Inquisitorial Squad with students from Slytherin and wears tweed in Slytherin green at the Quidditch match while sitting with them).

Umbridge developed into one of the most deplorable characters in the series. She began by secretly sending Dementors after Harry in an attempt to neutralize and discredit him. She also actively censored all word of the truth of Voldemort's return, especially at Hogwarts. In doing so, she unintentionally helped the Dark Lord and his followers without actually being a Death Eater herself.

Similar to Slytherins who believe that those with impure blood are inferior, Umbridge drafted anti-werewolf legislation while still at the Ministry aimed against "tainted" wizards such as the werewolf Remus Lupin, victims of circumstance who then find it difficult to find jobs and live normal lives. She also campaigned to have merpeople captured and tagged in her crusade against part-humans, and her prejudices even led to the attack against the half-giant Hagrid. (Appropriately, Umbridge's prejudices prove dangerous even to herself; when she insults the centaurs in their territory at the end of *Order of the Phoenix*, the centaurs react violently and capture her, though she is found the next morning, traumatized, but uninjured.)

Umbridge's time at Hogwarts is best exemplified by her merciless and sadistic punishments against students. She forces both Harry (repeatedly) and Lee Jordan to write "lines" as detention punishment, but in a far worse way than simply using quill and ink; they were forced to use a cruel black quill that magically caused the words they wrote to be cut into the skin on the backs of their hands and used their blood as the ink on the parchment. She disbands all clubs and, when Harry's Defense Against the Dark Arts club is discovered, Dumbledore takes the fall for him, leaving the power-crazy Umbridge in charge of the school. She tries to use Veritaserum on Harry to locate Dumbledore and Sirius. She grants Argus Filch permission to use corporal punishment on students (this is what finally drives Fred and George Weasley to leave the school before finishing the year, although by then they were looking for an excuse). She even attempts to use the unforgivable—not to mention illegal—Cruciatus Curse, a spell that inflicts excruiating pain, in order to extract information from Harry. She rewards some students for reporting

on others and authorizes them to act as enforcers of her rules. Umbridge, like a true Slytherin, uses any means necessary to get what she wants.

Is it any surprise that all the students who join Umbridge's Inquisitorial Squad belong to Slytherin? Conversely, Harry's Defense Against the Dark Arts club, "Dumbledore's Army," contains only Gryffindors, Hufflepuffs, and Ravenclaws (of course, no Slytherins were likely invited to join in the first place and for good reason: as a rule, they cannot be trusted).

Although we have no conclusive proof that Umbridge's boss, Cornelius Fudge, was a Slytherin, his ambition, his tendency to favor former Slytherin members such as Lucius Malfoy, his dislike of Dumbledore, his greed, and his addiction to power and privilege certainly make him a reasonable candidate. Although he initially seemed good-natured, Fudge, like Umbridge, helps Voldemort unwittingly by squashing all news of his return, discrediting Harry, and following the orders of a Death Eater in exchange for a tidy sum.

Clearly, there's little to recommend Slytherin or its members. So we're left to ask: Why does the House exist at all? Slytherin is a part of every one of us, as much as we all hate to admit it. Just like humans, not all wizards and witches are good. While the idea of the Wicked Witch or Evil Wizard may seem a bit stereotypical, any society without evil would be ridiculous. Children's books often include signposts to help young readers along, a position that the four Houses at Hogwarts perform admirably, but Slytherin provides more than an easy categorization and a red flag to a reader; it represents that side of our world that we don't like to acknowledge but must recognize nonetheless, because, thanks to human nature, it isn't going anywhere. We're human, and, as Dumbledore himself said, "'[H]umans do have a knack for choosing precisely those things that are worst for them'" (*Sorcerer's Stone* 297). Think of Slytherin's presence as a reminder. And watch your back.